TACKY

Finding God's Help
In Times of Crisis

by

Eloise Y. Lott

TACKY
by Eloise Y. Lott

Printed in the United States of America

ISBN 978-1-60791-347-4

Unless otherwise indicated, Bible quotations are taken from the King James Version of the Bible.

The names in the stories have been changed to protect confidentiality.

www.xulonpress.com

Tacky

Tacky

Book Dedication

I would like to dedicate this book in honor of my Savior,
Jesus Christ, Who has carried me through the many
heartaches and pains of this life.

The example of His Life, Death, and Resurrection
made the way for us (who by faith, accept Him
as our Savior).
His forgiveness gives us an opportunity to spend Eternity with Him.

Tacky

CHAPTER ONE

The beautiful, clear-blue water of Lake Bruin and the roots of an old cypress tree provided the perfect place for Tacky to sit and think while swooshing her little five-year-old legs and feet in the water. These old cypress roots served as a comfortable lap for Tacky's scrawny little body and as her favorite "thinkin' spot," and her "security hide-a-way" from her teasing, tormenting twin brothers.

Tacky always had many thoughts to straighten out in her impressionable young mind. She also tried various ways of coping with the inequality of a scrawny, five-year old with mischievous, eight-year-old,twin brothers.

Just that morning, Tacky, Todd and Rodd played in the back-yard tent. The boys had set it up to provide some shade from the hot Louisiana sun, when Mama came out on the porch and called, "How about some fresh-popped corn?" So, all three children dashed to the porch to get their share of this delicious treat.

"Shucks, Mama forgot to salt the corn," Todd complained as they got back into the tent to eat their treat.

"Tacky, how about runnin' inside to get the salt?"

"Okay, Todd. I'll go get it!" Tacky always wanted to gain the twins' approval, so she set her pan of corn down in the door of the tent and took off for the salt.

When she returned, her pan had been licked clean. Seeing the chickens pecking around the yard, Tacky murmured, "I'll bet them damn little chickens ate every bit of my popcorn!"

As Rodd and Todd left the tent, they bent doubled over with laughter, and Todd said,"Hey, Tacky. Here's some more corn. If you want some, come and get it!" Of course, they had emptied Tacky's corn into their own pans to tease her.

Tacky had all she could do to hold back the tears and anger she felt. Her contorted face told her frustration--she didn't see anything funny; but knowing the twins, she figured they had somthing else up their sleeve. She didn't have to wait long to find out just what.

Then, Rodd smiled sweetly at Tacky and said, "Tacky, this corn makes us thirsty, run in the house and get me and Todd a glass of water."

Still upset over their trick and laughter, she said, "Get it yourself; I'm not your slave!"

In response, Rodd's eyes beamed with mischief, as he grinned and said, "Wanta bet? I believe you'll be glad to get our water, for you see...if you refuse, we'll tell Mama about your cussin'."

Tacky thought to herself, *I didn't realize I was cussin'; I know I'll be in a lot of trouble with mama if she finds out. I never tell on the twins when they use bad words'cause I don't want to see them get a whipping!I feel their pain when that happens.*
So, as usual, Tacky did what the twins asked.

Tacky kicked at the water making ripples as she thought

Tacky

Gettin' the salt and water for the twins wasn't all that bad. It's just the way they use me, makin' me clean and polish their old muddy boots and shoes, because they always have somethin' on me.

The old cypress tree gave Tacky a measure of comfort and security she couldn't find anywhere else, and the peace of the beautiful water soothed her mind. The reflection of the trees in the water's edge created a lovely scene. But even there she had to be very careful the twins didn't know where she was, or they would slip up behind her and push her into the water or swim underneath the water, catch her feet and pull her in. Anytime they played in the lake, the twins watched her closely, and when she ventured out into the water up to her chin, they slipped up behind her and either ducked her or pulled her feet from under her. She always feared they would surely drown her some day.

That afternoon, Tacky came out of the house just as a marble came shootin' across the sandy yard at her feet. She stooped to pick it up. Todd, angry because he was losing the marble game, yelled, "Tacky-Lou, leave our marbles alone and get out of our way!"

"I'm not in your way, and I'm not botherin' your ol' marbles, and my name isn't Tacky Lou!" Tacky said as she stuck out her tongue at him.

Todd glared at her with anger. "Just for that, Smarty, I think I'll just pee on you," he yelled, as he started toward her, pretending to open his fly.

Tacky started runnin' and screamin'. Nothing was worse than being peed on. As she rounded the corner of the house, there stood Papa on the porch. Papa was a tall, straight man with keen, steel-blue eyes, and dark brown hair. A strict disciplinarian, Papa didn't put up with much foolishness.

"What's all this commotion?" He demanded.

Tacky didn't want to get Todd in trouble, but she knew she had to talk fast or get in trouble herself.

"Todd's tryin' to pee on me!" she cried.

Todd slid to a stop when he saw Papa, and Papa declared in his gruff, authoritative tone, "Boy, you'd better stop that foolishness. I'll take my knife and cut that thing off clean up to your belly."

Tacky didn't know if Papa would do that, but he sounded mighty convincing. Anyway, Todd stopped chasing her.

Although the twins dealt Tacky much misery, they also spent many happy times together playing in the woods and water, when they were not busy working in the cotton fields.

One of their favorite pastimes with the neighbor children was to gather in the woods and locate a hickory saplin' just the right size. Then they pulled it to the ground and coaxed Tacky to hold on near the top; at the count of three, everyone turned loose except Tacky.

"Hold on for dear life," they yelled as she swished into the air, screaming with a mixture of fear and delight. Tacky delighted being chosen for the hard or scary ventures, for that made the twins proud of her. When no one else would volunteer, Tacky always gave in. Nothing pleased her more than being in the twins' high esteem.

They also enjoyed collectin' alligator scales underneath the roots of the old cypress tree. The beautiful, rock-like scales had tiny little white pearl designs on the brown. Tacky couldn't swim well enough to gather the scales like the twins, but when no one was around, she would hold onto the cypress roots with one hand, take a deep breath, and stick her head underneath the water as she felt along the sandy bottom with her free hand for the scales.

One time when Lake Bruin flooded, a twelve-foot alligator washed up in a neighbor's yard. All the children gathered around to watch as the adults fastened a chain around it, hooked a mule to the chain to drag it off to the marshy swamp. It frightened the children to see it lunge and try to bite the men as they fastened the chain and then watch it dive for the heels of the mule as it was dragged away.

On Saturday afternoons after a hard week in the cotton fields, the whole family gathered at the lake for a fun-time. The twins wanted to teach Mama to dive. They demonstrated how easy it was, "All you have to do is run to the end of the divin' board, hold your hands together straight above your head, bounce up and down a couple of times, hold your breath and dive," Todd instructed.

While the twins coached her, Mama climbed unto the diving board, jumped up and down a few times, then lost her nerve and stepped back. When Papa laughed at her, her face got beet red, and with the twins cheering her on, she went back to the board with a glint of determination in her cool, brown eyes, she announced, you think I don't have the nerve? I'll show you, I'm no 'fraidy cat!' Papa grinned.

"Bravo, Mama!" The twins hollered.

As they counted, she sprang up and down, and at the count of three, in she jumped. Poor Mama, she had held her breath so long while jumping that she expelled it just before hitting the water...along with her false teeth! She came up coughing and spitting the water she swallowed. But she started to cry as she thought about her teeth. She knew Papa would never spend "hard earned money" for another set.

"Don't worry, Mama, we'll find your teeth," Todd consoled.

"Yeah, our persuadin' caused you to lose them, so don't worry, we'll find them." Rodd chimed.

They began diving, feeling along the bottom of the lake, searching for the teeth. Todd and Rodd spent the rest of the afternoon in the search, with family and neighbors all joining in, without any luck. Even the mischievous twins felt badly about Mama's loss.

Mama's mealtime struggle hurt Tacky. At first, she began to find things to do while the family ate, because chewing was such a slow, painful ordeal. Then, she suffered embarrassment because she slurred her speech; she also kept her hand over her mouth when anyone came around.

Each day when the family came in for dinner, the twins rushed to the lake to resume the hunt, while Mama, Teresa and Tacky put dinner on the table. Papa wasn't much help when he said, "You might as well give up, those teeth have washed away, or a turtle has swallowed them by now." Tacky grimaced at the thought of a turtle with Mama's pretty teeth.

Several weeks after the tragedy, the twins had hardly gotten out of sight, when Tacky heard screaming and hollering. She rushed to the door to see Todd racing to the house, and waving his hand in the air, yelling, "I found them; I found them!"

Rodd came right behind yellin' somethin'. They rushed in, asking,"Where's Mama?"

Mama walked in, "What's going on?" She asked. Todd rushed up to her, opened his hand, and there was Mama's bottom plate. Mama began to cry, the tears streaming down her cheeks, as she hugged the boys.

They started back to the lake, but Papa said," We've got to work in the field as soon as we finish eating."

Finding that plate had renewed the twins' interest, though, and they couldn't wait to resume the hunt.

A few days later, when the family came in at dark, the twins, as usual, rushed back to the lake while Papa, Bill and

Tacky

Frisk took care of the stock, and Mama milked ole Pet. Tacky and
Teresa made slaw, peeled tomatoes and onions and baked a pan of
cornbread on the old woodstove to go with the good vegetables left
from dinner.

While Mama strained the milk, the twins sauntered in quietly
and stood on either side of her. Mama looked suspiciously from one
to the other, smiling her mis-shaped smile with her top plate
still missing, and said, "What are you two up to now?"

They grinned, and said, "Oh, we've got a little surprise for
you."

"A surprise?" Mama stopped her work and looked at them.
Their grins grew broader. Rodd brought his hand from behind him
and held out her missing plate.

Mama hugged the boys against her breast as she cried. She
took the plate to the stove, took salt, soda, a blackgum tooth
brush and hot water and scrubbed her teeth until they they were
bright and shining. After rinsing them with cold water, she put
them into her mouth and smiled the sweetest smile Tacky ever saw.
We all enjoyed having Mama sit down to eat with the family again,
and not cover her mouth with her hand.

"I think we'd better say grace tonight," Papa said, and at
the end, he said, "and Lord, we thank You that the lost has been
found!" Everyone at the table joined the "AMEN" in a joyous
chorus.

"And thank You for sons who don't give up," Mama whispered,
looking at the twins with a wink and her warmest smile.

Seeing Mama eat with her family and smile during the entire
meal, and knowing that her slurred speech and empty mouth were
gone for good, gave the whole family a treat.

Tacky

CHAPTER TWO

Twenty years Mama's senior, Papa stood straight
and slim. His steel blue eyes could be as cold as a
blizzard on a winter morning, or as warm as the sunshine on a
clear day in June. A stern, hardworkin' farmer who
firmly believed in "earnin' your livin' by the sweat of your
brow," Papa taught all his children from the cradle
up, the importance of honest, hard work. He often quoted,
"The Lord abhors dishonest scales, but accurate weights are
His delight," (Proverbs 11:1).

He had five children when his wife died, the oldest only
three years younger than Mama. His three oldest children had
already married when he began dating Mama. Jessica and Teresa
were his two daughters that still lived at home.

Mama, a pleasantly plump, loving woman, had dark brown hair,
which she kept cut short, but immaculately clean. Her warm, brown
eyes were kind and affectionate. She had one son named Bill from
an earlier marriage (she had divorced this alcoholic, wife and
child-abusing, husband).

Papa's two daughters had long hair and wore their dresses
down to their ankles when Papa and Mama married.

14

Tacky

Not long after their marriage, Mama asked Jessica and Teresa
if they would like to have their long hair cut and their dresses
shortened like the other girls in school.

Their eyes lighted up, and a big smile spread across their
faces, then Jessica dropped her head and said, "I'm sure Papa
wouldn't like it."

"If I can work it out with him, would you like to have it
done?" Mama asked.

"Oh, YES!" They both chimed in.

Now, Papa was against such "frivolous things of the world."
But it wasn't long until Mama had talked him into allowing the
change. It was amazing the difference it made in Jessica and
Teresa's relationship with the other children at school.

Mama baked cakes and cookies to put in their lunch-pails, and
Papa complained, "You use more sugar in a month than my first wife
used in a year!"

"But none of it goes to waste...you and the children
certainly seem to enjoy it," she smugly reminded him.

Two years after their marriage, Mama gave birth to twin boys.
She thought Papa would be extremely proud of the twins since he
only had one son, but Papa didn't show his feelings much over
anything or anyone.

Three years later, Tacky came into the world as a premature,
three-pound baby. At the age of three, Tacky was still very
scrawny, but had eyes as big and blue as the Alabama Skies, and
auburn red hair. The Lord also blessed her with freckles as
plentiful and rusty as the spots on a leopard. The freckles earned
her the nickname, and brought many unkind comments like:

"Hi, Carrot-Top!"

"Did your Mom wash your face and forget to dry it?"

"Just when did your face begin rusting?"

"Is your hair really orange?"

Tacky

Tacky hated her red hair and freckles. She felt that God
must have really had it in for her to give her red hair, freckles,
and older twin brothers.

Papa and Mama owned a farm in North Alabama with a large
white house built near a tumblin' creek. The woods east of the
big house were something to see. Each season held its own extreme
beauty. In the spring, the honey suckle, rhododendron, grancy-
greybeard, violets, and sweet shrubs filled the woods with beauty
as well as captivating aromas.

Mama loved flowers and kept her garden and yards bordered
with multi-colored petunias, marigolds, zinnias, snapdragons,
bachelor buttons, phlox and a great variety of other flowers.

Papa planted a hedge around the border of the front
yard, which had grown into a beautiful frame for a picturesque
yard. He kept it neatly trimmed with a square top and sides; in
the spring, Mama sunned her mattresses and bedding out there
durin' spring-house-cleanin'. She was very particular about her
house and beds and would often remark, "Cleanliness is next to
Godliness."

Papa made a mop from a twelve-inch square board, with holes
bored in staggered rows. He pulled shucks through the holes and
tied them from the top side. Mama would take a hammer and break
up sandrock, spreading it all over the floor, then pour hot lye
soapsuds, over the floors and use the shuck mop to scrub them
clean. The children were called to draw water from the well near
the back porch as she rinsed the soapsuds and sandrock off the
floors, leavin' them bright, clean and sweet-smellin', an aroma
that made sleeping a dream.

One day, Papa heard about the prolific crops grown in
Louisiana and decided to go down and investigate. When he
returned, Tacky heard him say, "Martha, you oughta see that

cotton...I walked out in some fields where it was higher than my head. We could really make some money down there."

"Robert, do you really think we would make enough extra to pay for the move, the rent, and bein' away from our own home and family?"

"Ah, Martha, I know how you hate to leave our home and family, but you must realize that kin-folks don't make our livin', and we can draw rent off our place here, to off-set the rent we have to pay down there."

"I know Robert, but what if we move and then don't like it down there?"

"We can always move back."

Papa was very persuasive in his picturing of this land of prosperity! It sounded pretty much like the Land of Caanan to Mama, but she wasn't quite convinced that it wouldn't have its giants to overcome as well. But they had time to think about it, for they wouldn't be movin' until early spring. Papa seemed pretty much set on the move, so Mama began gatherin' flower and garden seeds, marking them so she would know what they were, if they did decide to move.

Jessica had fallen in love, and married just before Christmas. Mama sold cotton from the farm she had inherited from her father to buy Jessica a new coat to wear when she married. Papa thought her old one was good enough, but Mama wanted her to look nice and gave her the new coat. Jessica hugged Mama as tears bubbled up in her eyes. This was the first new coat she had ever owned. She always had to take the ones the two older sisters had outgrown.

After Christmas, Papa went down to St. Joseph, Louisiana, rented a farm and in the early spring moved the family to this fertile area.

Tacky

As Mama dug up the yard around her new home and planted the
seed she had so carefully saved, she would talk with Tacky, "I
grew these holly-hocks around the upper garden fence and in the
back yard near the smokehouse, 'back home.'

"Remember how beautiful these four-o-clocks looked late in the
afternoon around our back porch, near the well?"

"If these petunias do half as well here as they did 'back
home' we'll have a beautiful yard."

"Tacky heard so much about 'back home' that she was sure
it must have been the next thing to Heaven, or at least the
beautiful Garden of Eden, she had heard Mama read about.

Soon, Papa hired Frisk to help him on the farm. He was a
kind man, who made much over Tacky and her bright red hair. Even
though they were of different races, Tacky took to Frisk's
kind, understandin' ways, and when the torments of the twins
or the misunderstandings of family or friends hurt her sensitive
feelings, she always knew Frisk would understand. He didn't say
much, but Tacky could read the concern in his kind, black eyes,
and tender smile.

One day, Tacky and Todd were racing to see who could pick the
most cotton. Even though Tacky worked her scrawny little hands as
fast as she could, she couldn't keep up with Todd.

When the Postman stopped at the mailbox, Todd took his
picksack from his shoulder, and ran to get the mail. While he was
gone, Tacky picked her row up to where he had left his picksack.
Lookin' at the sack, which looked fuller than hers, even though
she had picked up with him, she decided it would be all right to
get a couple of hand-fulls of cotton from his sack; no one would
ever know. She looked around to be sure no one would see her..but
just as she put the first handful into her picksack, a voice
behind her said, "What do you think you are doin', Tacky?" She

jumped, looked up, her face as red as her hair, and saw Papa standing over her.

"You know that's stealin' don't you, young lady?"

"Yes, Sir!" Tacky whispered as tears spilled down her freckled cheeks.

"Tacky, do you realize your character is like the house you live in...when you lie or steal...it's like tearin' shingles off the roof...when the rains and storms come, it deteriorates the house until it is finally destroyed?" Papa emphasized his lecture by wearin' a cotton stalk out across Tacky's scrawny legs and backside.

Tacky could see her character fallin' apart, and felt that her little body wasn't far behind. She remembered... *'The Lord abhors dishonest scales, but accurate weights are His delight.'*

"I wonder if the Lord will ever forgive me for all the things I seem to be doin'...cussin', stealin'?" She whispered to herself after Papa left, and the tears continued to stream down her five-year-old freckled face.

Frisk, the one who had lovingly given Tacky her nickname, had witnessed the whippin' and lecture. When he picked up with her, he whispered, "Dry, them tears, Tacky, before you have more rusty spots." He reached over and patted her shoulder and winked at her, smilin'. She tried to smile through her tears. His kind understanding meant everything to her.

Tacky

CHAPTER THREE

Not long after arriving in St. Joseph, Mama heard of a
lady who lived down the road from her who was very sick. Rumors
were that she wasn't expected to live, because no one could get
her to eat.

"Tacky, would you like to go with me to check on Miss
Liza, whom I've been told is very sick?"

"Oh, Yes Ma'am!"

Tacky's eyes beamed. She always got excited when Mama
was goin' to help someone.

"You'll have to be very quiet, for this lady needs all
the quiet and rest she can get," Mama cautioned.

"Oh I will, Mama. Do we get to walk through the woods?"

Tacky liked to explore the woods, so this was a special
treat.

"Well, I hadn't thought about it, but I guess there is a
short-cut through the woods." Mama smiled at Tacky.

"Oh thank you, Mama. I just love hoppin', and skippin'
through the woods, huntin' sweet-williams, black-eyed susans,
and, Oh! the buck-eye is so pretty now."

"Yes, the woods are lovely in the spring, and

Tacky

Tacky, I don't think I have ever seen anyone that gets such a thrill from strolling through them as you do...but this is not a treasure hunt...it's a mercy trip!"

"Yes, Ma'am, I understand....You get as much enjoyment from being helpful in times of need as I do from wanderin' through my beloved woods, huntin' the many treasures that lay hidden underneath the leaves, or behind a bush or rock."

Mother smiled at Tacky's wisdom coming from such a scrawny little five-year old, as she came skipping over to squeeze her arm, laying her face against it to show her appreciation for this great treat.

About that time Tacky's eyes spotted a beautiful bunch of violets. "Oh Mama, this will make a dainty little bouquet for the sick lady. Can I pick them for her?"

"She will probably be too sick to realize we are even there, but you can take them if you wish." Mama didn't want to spoil Tacky's joy in giving.

Mama walked up to the door of the small log cabin and tapped gently on the door. A young girl came to the door.

"I'm Martha Mayberry, and this is my daughter we call Tacky. We have just recently moved into the neighborhood. I heard a sick lady lived here that might need some help."

"Yes'm, she's Liza and she's most gone already."

"I'm Katrina, folks call me Kat. I'm Liza's cousin."

"Is it all right if I come in and see Liza?" Mama asked gently.

"It's all right...but I don't know what good anyone can do. You can come in, though, if you want to," Kat said and stepped aside.

"Tacky, you had better wait outside." Mama said.

"Here are some pretty violets, I'd like to give Miss Liza," Tacky said, holding the violets out to Kat.

Tacky

Kat smiled at Tacky, took the violets inside and put
some water in a small jar and arranged them in it. She came
back to the door holding them out for Tacky to see.

"They do make a nice little bouquet, don't they?" Kat
said as she smiled at Tacky for her thoughtfulness.

"Yes, Ma'am. I love flowers, especially the beautiful
wild flowers God planted all over the woods," Tacky said
with enthusiasm.

Mama went to Liza's bed, put her hand on Liza's fevered
brow, and spoke softly. "Liza, I'm your new neighbor, Martha
Mayberry. I have come to help you get well."

Liza just moved her head and moaned.

Mama came to the door. "Kat, has Liza had a doctor
check her?"

"Yes'm, he said she had pneumonia and might not make it.
He left some medicine, but I can't get her to swallow any of
it."

"Do you care if I try to doctor her with some of my home
remedies?"

"No'm, don't look like she's gonna make it nohow." Kat
said as tears trickled down her dark cheek. Mama put her arm
around her..."Now, Now, don't cry. We're going to help Liza.
With the Lord's help she'll be better soon...just you wait
and see!"

"I sure hope so." Kat said, dryin' her eyes on the
sleeve of her dress.

"Kat, I would like some bakin' soda, a pan of room
temperature water, a clean wash cloth and a towel. Does she
have any any clean gowns?"

"No'm I don't believe so. I put the last clean one on
her this afternoon, the other one was so wet. I haven't had
a chance to wash...I was afraid to leave her alone."

22

"Tacky, do you think you could find your way home?"

"Oh yes, Ma'am!" Tacky's eyes shone as she knew she would be
be trusted to do a big errand.

"Listen carefully...run home, look in the bottom dresser
drawer in mine and Papa's bedroom and bring a clean gown, and
several sheets, while I bathe Liza."

"Yes, Ma'am!" Tacky's little heart swelled with pride to
think Mama trusted her for such an important task.

"Tacky, please be careful, but hurry!" Mama cautioned as
Tacky took off in a run.

"I will, Mama." She yelled over her shoulder as she
went skippin' down the lane.

Kat went to fetch the supplies Mama had asked for. She
watched as Mama put some soda in the water and began spongin'
Liza's hot body. She gently rubbed a small portion of her
body at a time, covering her with a thick bath towel to keep
her body warm. She took the medicine bottle, read the
directions, got a teaspoon, poured some medicine in it, and
put it to Liza's lips. She did not respond. Mama asked Kat to
hand her another teaspoon with which she tried to open her
mouth a little. She finally got it slightly opened, and
trickled the medicine into her mouth, then stroked her neck
muscles gently until she felt her swallow. She had Kat bring
some fresh spring water, and trickled a few drops down her
throat.

Before long, Tacky came runnin' in all out of breath with the
gowns and sheets.

"Thank you, Tacky," Mama smiled and slipped the fresh
gown on Liza, and she and Tacky turned Liza on her side,
while Kat pulled the wet sheet and rolled it up to her back.
Mama sponged her back off, rubbed it with alcohol, then
powdered it with baby powder, then put the fresh sheet on

half the bed. Mama folded one sheet in several folds to make a pad, and put that on top the fresh sheet. She and Kat lifted Liza up slightly while Tacky pulled the wet sheet from under her, and the fresh one over the bed. Mama pulled the clean gown down, straightened the covers and spread the fresh dry sheet, gently over her.

"Kat, I know you don't like to leave Liza alone, to do the washin'. Would you be afraid for Tacky to sit with her, while you get the washin' started, and I run home and kill one of my big, fat, Rhode Island Reds, which I moved here from 'back home', and make some broth to feed Liza?"

"That would be nice, but I don't think you can get her to eat anything," Kat said doubtfully.

"I think I might get a little down her...it is worth a try anyway. If you don't mind," Mama said convincingly.

"Oh, no, Ma'am, I don't mind."

"Tacky, you must sit very quietly beside Liza's bed. If she begins to talk or move much, go to the door and call Kat. Do you understand what an important task this is for you?"

"Oh, yes, Ma'am!" Tacky's heart swelled with pride to be so useful in this important endeavor. "I'll take real good care of her for you and Kat, Mama!" she promised.

"I'm sure you will, dear." Mama said as she left.

Kat gathered up all the wet clothes and washed and boiled all the sheets, gowns, towels and wash cloths. She rinsed them, and hung them out to dry.

Tacky kept a silent vigil at Liza's bedside. Gently patting her hand every little while. She was very excited to be included in this important job.

Soon Mama returned with the chicken broth, and some more sheets, gowns and some pads she had made from some worn out sheets. She had taken the good parts of the sheets and sewed

them together in large pads, so Liza could be kept dry
without always having to change the sheets.

"Is there any change in Liza?" Mama asked hopefully.

"No'm, she's slept or coughed all the time you and Kat have
been gone," Tacky volunteered.

"The sleep will do her good, and I sure hope we'll soon
be able to get this cough stopped." Mama smiled at Tacky.

When the broth cooled enough, Mama poured a little
in a cup, took a spoon and carried it to Liza's bedside.

"Liza, this is Martha, I have brought you some delicious
chicken broth...just smell how good it smells." Mama held
the cup of broth near Liza's nostrils so she could smell the
invigorating aroma.

"Doesn't it smell delicious?" There was no response.

"Open your mouth and taste this good nourishin' broth.
It will make you feel better."

Liza didn't respond in any way, but Mama patiently
worked with the spoon until she was able to get her teeth
slightly apart. She let a few drops of warm broth trickle
into her mouth...then stroked her throat muscles. She worked for
hours just getting a few drops at a time down. she talked to Liza
using kind and encouraging words and finally got half
a cup of the broth down. Mama was very elated, at this great
accomplishment.

Kat couldn't believe anyone would be so jubilant over such a
small accomplishment, but Mama knew it was a beginning.

"Kat, I must go back to fix supper for my family. In
about half an hour I want you to try to get a few more drops
of this broth down Liza's throat. Work very patiently, so as
not to strangle her. Her medicine will be due again in about
two hours, but I'll be back by then."

When Mama returned she brought a bottle of her home-canned blackberry juice.

After trickling the medicine down Liza's throat, she poured a little of the blackberry juice into a small glass and trickled a few drops into her mouth.

"Kat, who is goin' to sit with Liza tonight?"

"Miz Martha, we don't have nobody. I get up and down with her, and get what sleep I can."

"Do you mind if I come back and stay during the night? She is very sick, and it is so important that she have her medication on a regular schedule. Her temperature is down just a little, and I think if she keeps getting the medicine, and a little liquid, she'll begin to improve."

"I sure would be glad to have you stay. It's scary that she might die with only me here." The tears fell down Kat's cheeks.

Mama patted Kat's shoulder and gave her a sympathetic squeeze. "I know it is, Kat. Don't worry, I'll be back."

"Come on, Tacky; it's about your bedtime."

When they arrived at home, Mama said, "Tacky, go wash yourself, eat supper, and get ready for bed. I need to talk with Papa."

While Tacky was eating, she heard Mama say, "Papa, Liza is certainly going to die unless someone takes care of her. Kat is doing the best she can but she is so young, she just doesn't understand how to care for a very sick person."

"About eight o'clock, I'd like you to walk me back, and I will sit with her, and give her medication regularly and keep her warm and dry."

"How are you goin' to get your work done and sit up all nightover there?" Papa asked.

"I can sleep some, I'm sure. Don't worry about me, I will get my work done, but most of all I want to help Liza

Tacky

recover."

"You'll probably make yourself sick waitin' on her, and
may even cause us to lose a crop." Papa was very much against
Mama's new project.

"Now Robert, you know that the Lord expects us to do what we
can for our neighbors, and Liza will surely die if something isn't
done, and done in a hurry."

"Well, I don't see that it's your responsibility...after all
you are new in the neighborhood."

"Well, no one else has done it, and I can't see why I'm not
as responsible as anyone."

"I know there's no need to argue, when you get that
determined look in your eyes, so let me know when you're ready,"
Papa said.

Mama smiled at Papa, walked over kissed his forehead and
patted his shoulder. "Thank you!" She whispered.

"Tacky, you and the twins get your baths and get ready for
bed, before I leave. I'll be back in time to cook breakfast."

"Teresa can cook breakfast. It's time she did more cookin'
anyway, she needs to be learnin'," Papa said.

Teresa didn't answer, she enjoyed reading and just looked up
from her book long enough to let them know that she knew she was
being talked about.

Mama mixed some toddy and honey for cough medicine. Liza
coughed so much she couldn't get any rest day or night. Mama
kissed Rodd, Todd and Tacky goodnight and tucked them in their
beds and gathered up many supplies to take with her.

Kat was relieved when Mama returned with her supper; she ate
and went to bed.

Mama was busy most of the night changing the pads underneath
Liza, trickling the cough mixture down her throat, and giving her
medicine regularly. About 3:00 a.m. Liza began to breathe a

27

little more freely, and finally stopped coughing long enough to
drift into a deep sleep.

Early in the morning Kat awoke, got up, dressed and came
in to see about Liza. She was relieved that she was still alive.

"Kat, do you think you can care for Liza while I run home
for a little while?"

"Yes'm, if you'll tell me what to do."

"Just keep the juice goin' down, when she awakes. I'll bring
some applesauce and some chicken soup when I come back. This will
give a little more nourishment than just the broth and juice."

Kat timidly walked over to Mama, put her arm over her
shoulder and said, "Thank you, Miz Martha, for what you done last
night. I got the best sleep I've had in weeks."

Mama put her arm around the slender, young girl, squeezed her
and smiled as she said, "I'm sure you needed it, Child!"

Mama soon increased Liza's meals to chicken and dumplin's,
chicken and rice, creamed potatoes, home-canned peaches and jello,
until she was soon sitting up in bed, and saying "I'm starving!"

This was a great day for Mama, Tacky, and Kat. Mama and Kat
began walking Liza around the room to help her gain some strength
in her shaky legs. Tacky picked a fresh bouquet of flowers each
day to bring her.

Liza said, "Tacky, this is the first time in my life that
anyone has ever brought me flowers."

This thrilled Tacky, for she loved scampering through the
woods to find the beautiful wild flowers growing there. To be able
to share them with someone was a great treat to her as well as for
her recipient.

"Miz Martha, you have certainly been an angel of mercy.
I know you will have staws in yo crown one day for all you done
for me," Liza said, thoughtfully.

Tacky

　　Liza was lookin' at Mama with a glow of deep appreciation in her dark eyes. A bond had grown between the two that the difference in their race didn't matter. Many times after Liza recuperated, she came to help Mama with canning, quilting, and whatever she could assist Mama with.

Tacky

CHAPTER FOUR

Mama always went to milk before the rest of the family were
up. One morning she put out feed for the cow and sat down to
milk. Papa had just purchased a young bull who was in the same
pasture as the cow. He ran up, pushed the cow away, and proceeded
eating her feed. Mama tried to run him off, then he turned on
her, butted her to the ground and with his sharp horns, began
goring her and rollin' her over the pasture. Mama began to scream
for help. Frisk was in the barn loft, pitchin' hay down for the
stock. He heard Mama's screams, ran to look out and saw what was
happening; he threw his pitchfork out the hayloft, and jumped to
the ground, grabbed the pitchfork and ran to scare the bull away
from Mama. The bull pawed the ground and turned on Frisk, but he
jabbed him with the pitchfork and run him into the other pasture
and fastened the gate. Then he ran back to see how badly Mama was
hurt.

Mama was badly bruised, and had several ruptured blood
vessels in her legs.

"Thank the Lord you were close by, Frisk. I would have been
killed by that mean bull if you hadn't been here. I sure
appreciate your help."

"Yes'm, Miz Martha, I am sure thankful I was close enough to help, for you sho has been a blessin' to our people."

Papa never took the chance of the bull being in Mama's milking area anymore. Each evening he fastened him in another part of the pasture and left him there until after milking time next morning.

After some time, several neighbors became close friends with Papa and Mama. One day when Mama, Tacky, Mrs. Powell, and her young son, H.L., were going to visit Mrs. Peabody, Mrs. Powell told H.L (who was always asking for something to eat everywhere he went), "H.L., I'm fixing you something to eat before we leave, and if you ask for something at Mrs. Peabody's. I'm going to give you the whipping of your life."

When they arrived at Mrs. Peabody's, she was churning butter. When she finished, she took up the butter, washed all the milk out, made a beautiful cake of delicious, firm, yellow butter which she placed on a saucer, and took the butter paddle and designed a pretty flower design on top and placed it in her pie safe. She poured the fresh churned buttermilk into gallon jars, screwed the lids on tightly and let H.L. and Tacky help her fasten a rope around the neck of the jugs and lower them into a nearby spring, to keep them cool.

When they returned to the house, before settling down to visit with Mama and Mrs. Powell, she said, "H.L. and Tacky, how about a glass of milk and some fresh-baked cookies?"

Tacky thanked her and declined the treat.

H.L. said, "YES, MA'AM! I'd sure love to have some"...then seeing the look on his Mother's face, he hastily added, "but I'd die before I'd ask for any!"

Mrs. Powell just covered her face and shook her head. Mrs. Peabody smiled at Mrs. Powell and poured H.L. a glass of milk and placed a hefty stack of cookies on a saucer before him, and said, "Help yourself, son, a growin' boy needs plenty of food," She smiled and winked at him. He grinned his appreciation as he devoured a cookie.

Montie, Mrs. Peabody's daughter, came in from another neighbor's, and she and Tacky went out to play, telling H.L. to come out when he finished eating.

Tacky

CHAPTER FIVE

    Mama's longing for her family, 'back home' increased
daily. Tacky would see her as she watched for the postman,
hoping for a letter from home. One day when they were in the
cottonfield, Tacky saw the postman stop and asked if she
could go get the mail. Papa told her to be careful and not
lose any of it. Tacky had learned what a letter from home
looked like, even though she couldn't read. When there
wasn't one in the box, she wanted Mama to enjoy one so badly,
that she went to the house pulled a chair up to the old
fireboard where Mama always put her 'letters from home.' She
couldn't quite reach them, so she got down and got the Sears
Roebuck Catalog and put it on the chair, climbed on top of
it, and by stretching with all her might was able to reach a
letter from home. She tucked it under her arm until she could
climb down, then took off down to the cotton patch waving it in
the air, calling, "Oh Mama, a letter from home, a letter from
home." Mama jerked her picksack off and came running to meet
Tacky. She took the letter, and did not notice that the end
had been carefully cut out. (This was how she always opened
her letters when she was at the house) She ripped it open

from the other end and began reading. "They told me that
last time." She said as she read along. "They've already
told me that." She said as she continued reading. "Humm,
wonder why ....?" She stopped looked at the postmark on the
envelope and said,

"That's an old letter, you went to the house and got, Tacky.
You little devil!" she said as she threw the letter to the ground.
Papa had been standing by, listening, and burst out laughing, and
Mama began to cry.

"Well, it was a letter from home, Martha," Papa said
laughing. Mama didn't appreciate Papa's humor, and went back
to picking cotton while the tears continued to fall.

Tacky felt so bad about hurting Mama; she meant it to help.
Frisk, who had witnessed the dilemma, picked up with Tacky,

"She knows you meant it for good, Tacky, she's just
homesick."

When crops were finally harvested, Papa said to Mama,

"Martha how would you like to go home for a short visit?"
Mama's eyes lit up like the Fourth of July Fireworks. She grabbed
Papa, hugged his neck and said, "Really? When?"

Tacky, unable to remember back home very well, was
anxious to see all the things she had heard so much about.

Papa built a frame for his pick-up truck and bought a
tarpaulin to cover it. He built seats behind the
cab and down the sides of the truck bed. Mama padded them
with folded quilts for the children to sit on. She
fried chickens, sausages and ham, made a big batch of her
delicious, homemade biscuits, some teacakes, and packed all the
food in a big box. She packed clothes for everyone; then, after
the truck was loaded, they started on their journey early the next
morning to go 'back home!'

Mama and Papa rode in the cab of the truck. Teresa,

Tacky

Bill, the Twins and Tacky rode in the back. Before the sun
was up, they were well on their way. Teresa, as usual, had
her book to read, and as soon as it was daylight, she became
deeply engrossed in reading and paid no attention to the
others' bickering.

About the middle of the morning, Tacky felt the urge to
use the bathroom. Papa never wanted to be disturbed by
stopping when they were on a trip, so she put it off as long
as she possibly could, (which was a big mistake). When she
felt she could wait no longer, she tapped on the window of the
cab, and told them she needed to use the toilet and couldn't
wait. Papa thought this was just an excuse to
stop, so he kept driving. Soon she began to cry, for the
urge was becoming too strong to ignore.

Rodd pecked on the window and yelled, "Tacky needs to
use the bathroom!"

Papa yelled back, "It's too early to stop; she can wait
a while longer."

Tacky doubled over holdin' her stomach, sobbin' "I can't
wait!"

Todd relayed the message, but Papa replied, "We'll stop
after while. She'll just have to wait."

Bill felt sorry for Tacky and said, "Don't
worry about it, if you can't wait, you just can't wait. He's
been given fair warnin', so go ahead and tee tee in your
panties."

"It's more than tee, tee," sobbed Tacky.

Rodd beat on the cab..."Tacky couldn't wait...Shooooo...
you'll have to stop."

Finally, Papa pulled off the side of the road, near a
lovely stretch of tumblin' water. Mama came back to check on
things. Rodd and Todd held their noses, saying,

Tacky

"Shooooooooo!!!!"

Bill said, "Mama, Tacky couldn't help it; she gave
plenty of warning, but Papa wouldn't stop."

"I know." Mama replied, "Here, Tacky, let me see just
what you have done."

"Not here in front of everybody," Tacky cried. Mama
lifted her out of the truck, pulled down her panties, and
said, "Well, she has messed a little." The twins began to
snicker.

Tacky's little freckled face blazed with embarrassment.
Mama led her to the creek, removed her panties, got
some soap, talcum powder, and a towel from the truck cab, then
washed the panties in the clear cold water. Once they were clean,
she used them to wash Tacky. She dried her off with the towel,
powdered her and handed her some dry panties.

After Mama helped Tacky back into the truck, Tacky couldn't
look at the twins, who were still snickering and holding
their noses.

Mama returned to the cab, and Rodd whispered, "Well, she
messed a little."

Todd snickered, "Yeah, just a little. Smelled like a lot to
me."

Then both exploded with laughter. Bill slid closer to Tacky,
put his arm around her, and said, "Don't pay any attention to
those ugly brothers."

When they arrived in Alabama, every time they visited new
relatives, one of the twins would make it a point to get Tacky
in a crowd of people and look at her and say, "Well...she
messed a little." Then he'd take off runnin' and snickerin'.
Tacky's face would blush as red as her hair and she could
feel the heat going down her body to the tips of her toes.
She avoided the relatives as much as possible when the twins

were near.

Uncle Kent and Aunt Ava (Mama's brother and wife), lived
in Collinsville, and when they visited them, Aunt Ava went to
the kitchen and brought out three whole bananas for the Twins and
Tacky. Tacky couldn't believe they received a whole
banana apiece. She was used to having one banana divided
among the three of them, and if the twins divided it, she got
a much smaller third, because, as the twins said, "You're
littler." She looked at Mama to see if it was all right to
take a whole one. Mama smiled and nodded that it was. This
was Tacky's very first whole banana, and she thought Aunt Ava
was wonderful and must be very rich.

Another first came when they visited Mama's cousin
on Lookout Mountain. The peddler was just pulling away from
Cousin Regie Morris' house when they arrived. She bought some
beautiful pastel, blue, pink, yellow and green
bubble gum. She let the Twins and Tacky pick out their
favorite colors. The trip created many fond memories as well
as a few embarrassing ones for Tacky.

The following spring, Tacky was sick with a sore mouth and
couldn't eat anything but crackers soaked in milk and scraped
apples. The doctor said she had thrush. Her mouth was so
sore everything hurt. She lay on a cot in the living
room watching Mama piece quilt blocks. She wanted some
blocks to sew on too, and begged Mama to give her some. Mama
cut out a few pieces and gave Tacky a needle and thread, thinking
it was only a passing fancy and would soon be tossed aside,
but Tacky pieced them together faithfully. When Papa came in for
lunch, she showed him the block she had pieced. He bragged on it,
and said, "Tacky, when you get enough blocks to make a whole
quilt, I will buy some bright red material for you to put it
together with." Mama smiled for she and Papa both thought his

Tacky

money was safe. They were sure Tacky's interest would fade, but
Tacky liked a challenge. Every time she felt like sitting up for a
little while, she faithfully pieced on her quilt.

    Several weeks later when Papa came in for lunch, Tacky had
her blocks spread out on the bed to show him she had enough for
her quilt, and was ready for the red material so she could sew her
blocks together.

    Papa was shocked. "Tacky, I had no idea you would stay with
the work long enough to piece a whole quilt, but you have and the
first time I am in town I'll get that material I promised. Just
think, you pieced a whole quilt before you were six years old."
Papa seemed proud of her,and that thrilled her. She could hardly
wait for him to bring the material home so she could sew her
blocks together.

    One rainy day, she and Mama were working on their quilts
when they saw the postman stop at the mailbox. Mama picked
up an old coat and spread it over her head and went to get
the mail. She stopped on the porch to shake the raindrops
off the coat and opened her letter to read. When she came in
she was crying.

    "What's wrong, Mama?" Tacky always felt upset when her
mother cried.

    "Aunt Ava's dead," She said.

    Tacky sobbed,"Oh Mama, I'll never get another whole banana."

Tacky

CHAPTER SIX

After three years in Louisiana, Papa decided the "Grass on
the other side of the pasture wasn't quite as green as it had
appeared in the beginning." He would never admit it, but Mama had
been right in her thinking. There just wasn't enough extra money
in the prolific crops to pay for being away from home.

Teresa became quite interested in one of the neighbor boys,
so Papa thought it best to get her away. His other daughters had
married very young, and he didn't want Teresa to copy them. So he
began making arrangements to move 'back home.'

The family renting Papa's farm couldn't move immediately, but
Papa found a little house near Mama's youngest brother, and moved
the family back to Alabama. He entered the children in school and
went back to finish gathering his crops.

Aunt Sadie and Uncle Mart lived near a little creek.
Each Saturday afternoon, Aunt Sadie lined up her children near the
spring to wash their hair. She washed each of them in turn,
dipped water from the spring, and poured it over their heads to
rinse. The yells and screams could be heard far and wide all over
the countryside. On Sunday Morning, they looked so pretty with

their blond hair shining as they lined up on the church pews for
Sunday School.

One Saturday, Tacky timidly asked, "Aunt Sadie, would you
mind if I join the hair washing today?"

"Goodness no, Child. One more won't bother me." She smiled
and hugged Tacky.

Tacky got in line near the front, for she didn't believe
anything could be as bad as the others made it sound. And their
hair always looked so pretty when they finished. Tacky wanted hers
to look pretty like that. Mama always took warm water from the
reservoir on the wood stove to wash and rinse her children's hair,
but there would never be enough warm water to go around with Aunt
Sadie's group.

When Tacky's turn came, Aunt Sadie washed, rubbing the scalp
good with the ends of her fingers and a good shampoo, then dipped
the water from the spring for the rinsing. When that cold, clear
spring water hit her head, it took her breath away so fast that
she couldn't even scream...all she could do was shake like a leaf
in the wind. She never thought the screams were fake again.   If
that happened in modern times, when child abuse was well known,
she felt certain Aunt Sadie would've been arrested. Every time
Tacky remembered that hair washing, cold chills ran up and down
her spine.

The renters moved out just before Christmas, and moving back
home for Mama was like the Children of Israel going back to
Jerusalem after seventy years of Babylonian Captivity. Complete
Joy! It was the best Christmas in three years, for everyone
except Teresa. She seemed to be rather sad and more alone than
usual.

The Twins and Tacky changed schools and became settled at
home once again. Tacky wanted to learn everything the twins
learned. She dreamed of getting a good education.

When chopping and hoeing endless rows of cotton and corn, she
dreamed of someday working in a hospital or an office away from
the hot blistering sun. She was determined that she wouldn't
spend the rest of her life in such back-breakin' work.

They had a beautiful, tumbling creek near the house. Giant
oak trees extended their branches to welcome all who came near.
The children swam in the clear, cold water. It served both as a
refreshing enjoyment after a hard day in the field, and also as a
bath tub. After the long, hot hours in the field, the children
took off to the creek with a bar of soap, a bath rag, and a towel.

The woods were filled with an array of beautiful flowers
which refreshed the soul as much as the clean, cool water
refreshed the body. These woods became Tacky's childhood
paradise.
Jake, a neighbor boy just a couple of years younger than Tacky,
would come over, and they made playhouses on the beautiful flat
rocks in the woods. They built rock stoves and furniture, and
decorated their home with violets, sweet williams, honeysuckles,
sweet shrubs, rhodendhron or grancy graybeard. Their home was
always blessed with the fragrant smell of the beautiful wild
flowers, and their floors were carpeted with the lovely green moss
that grew near the creek banks. The woods held such an array of
beauty that it was no trouble to find any type of bouquet they
desired. Tacky didn't wonder that Mama wanted to come back home.

Tacky didn't know much about God in those days, but she felt
a sense of peace among the swaying trees as the gentle breeze
blew, sifting sunlight through the swaying branches overhead,
splintering it into thousands of diamonds that reflected on the
creek. In such a magnificent array of beauty, her heart soared
like an eagle.

The singing birds gave forth such peace and calm that it
erased all her childish worries and fears. That became her source

of peace and security as the old cypress had on the banks of Lake
Bruin.

Many years before, there was a sawmill at the top of the hill
above the swimming hole. A huge pile of sawdust was still there.
The twins built a sled and cut out a smooth path down the hill to
the creek, then covered it with sawdust. One got on the sled, and
the other gave it a push. It flew down the steep hill into the
creek. If it had enough speed, it soared over the water and
crossed to the opposite bank.

They spent many happy hours at the sawdust pile when they
didn't have to be in the fields or in school.

Occasionally, they would let Tacky slide down, but more often
they would both get on the sled and have her push them off the
hill. They helped by pushing with their feet along the sides
until they were started, then pulled up their feet and rode down
together.

Teresa soon met a young man named Peter Kratz and became
interested in him. He came to see her riding in a buggy pulled by
a beautiful horse. Todd and Rodd dealt her some embarrassing
moments during her courting days. They came close enough for
Teresa and her boy friend to hear them, and put their hand under
their armpits, and swung down their arms to make it sound like a
horse breaking wind. Then they ran off snickering and laughing,
saying,"That old horse is something else!"

Soon, Teresa and Peter were engaged. Tacky didn't know if
Teresa was marrying him to get away from the torment of the twins,
but she knew she'd miss her sister. She idolized Teresa, and
anything she did was just about perfect as far as Tacky was
concerned.

Tacky enjoyed reading and worked hard in school, because she
knew she had to study to make her dreams come true. Papa didn't
put much stock in more than a sixth grade education.

Tacky

He said, "As long as a person can read, write, and figure the price of a bale of cotton at a given price per pound, what more schooling is needed?" It bothered Tacky that Rodd and Todd had to quit school when they finished the sixth grade. Rodd bought books for the seventh, but Papa kept him out for work so much that he wasn't able to keep up with his school work. Finally, he became discouraged and quit.

Tacky kept dreaming of the day she'd finish high school and get a good job. Papa thought a penny spent for anything other than necessities was wasted, so Tacky didn't like to ask for anything. She didn't want to depend on someone else for things she needed or wanted.

Tacky

CHAPTER Seven

In the spring of 1936, just before school was out, Tacky
found a bad sore on her left leg. It began to spread until Papa
had to take her to the doctor. Visiting a doctor was almost
unheard of in her family.

Dr. Brannon gave her some white ointment to apply to the
infected area, and it soon began to heal. But, a short time after
it healed, another boil erupted until Tacky began having one boil
after another.

When school was out and the cotton and corn crops were ready
to chop and thin, Tacky experienced terrible pain from the boils
on her legs, arms, and different areas of the body. Every new
boil seemed to come in a worse spot than the one before. One time
she counted sixteen boils.She wondered if she was going to have
the same trouble Job had in the Bible.

One Friday, Tacky was choppin' cotton and crying over a
boil in the bend of her left knee. Every time the hoe hit the
ground, pail shot through her leg. The knee was so swollen she
couldn't straighten her leg.

Tacky

Papa never allowed anyone to stop work due to moderate pain, so Tacky kept on working and crying. By mid-afternoone, her body burned up with fever, and her whole body ached.

"You should see about Tacky, Papa," Bill said. "She's a sick little girl."

Papa walked over to check on Tacky, he said, "Ah, I think that red face is from the hot sun and from squalin' so much, but your foot and leg look pretty badly swollen. I guess you can go to the house, but before going to bed, go to Mrs. Peete's and get milk for supper, for we'll be workin' late, and for goodness sake, stop that squalin' before you go over there."

Tacky hobbled to the house, wishing she could stop crying, but the pain was excruciating. She wished Papa understood how badly it hurt. She didn't like to complain, for more than anything in the world, she wanted Papa to be proud of her.

But, she'd never felt such pain before. When she finally made it home, she drew two buckets of water from the well at the corner of the house, and took them to the smokehouse where they had a square hole dug in the dirt floor to keep milk and butter cool in hot weather.

She was so sick from the pain that she began to vomit, and just lay on the cool grass, until she could get over some of the nausea. She finally made herself get up to go after the milk. That half mile seemed like an eternity away. Several times she would have to prop herself against a tree alongside the road to keep from passing out.

When Mrs. Peete saw her she said, "Goodness Child! What in the world's wrong with you?"

Tacky showed her the boil behind her knee, which had swollen to the size of a small golf ball and had red streaks running down her leg. "But this leg, (pointing to her right leg,) hurts worse than that one," she said, and Mrs. Peete noticed that Tacky's

45

Tacky

right ankle was terribly swollen and also had red streaks running
up from it.

"Tacky, you shouldn't be hobbling around. Besides, you're
burnin' up with fever.What does your Father mean by sending you
after milk when you're sick as a dog? You should be in bed or in
a hospital!"

"He doesn't realize how I hurt." Tacky defended him.

"Well, as soon as you get home, go right to bed and get off
your feet and legs, Tacky. I know you are in terrible pain.
If I had anything here that would carry you, I wouldn't let you
walk another step."

"Thank you!" Tacky sobbed. Thank you for the milk."
When she finally made it home, Tacky had to lie on the grass
before she could manage to draw more water to pour into the
dug-out. She finally put the jug of milk in the hole, placed
a big rock on top of it to keep it from turning over when she
put more water around it. Then she placed the wooden lid over
the hole, and hobbled, half-crawled to the house.

Falling across the bed, she cried bitterly. Knowing how
dirty she was from working in the field, she dragged herself up to
sponge off with some water before putting on her pajamas. Then she
took two aspirin with a little water to cool her temperature, and
ease her splitting headache and aching body.

But the aspirin came up as quickly as they went down. She
vomited all over the kitchen floor. *Oh, what a mess,* she thought.
*I can't leave this for Mama to clean up; she'll be so tired when
she comes in.*

She dipped some warm water out of the reservoir and
sprinkled some soap on the floor and scrubbed it with the broom,
then rinsed it good, leaning against the wall several times to
keep from keeling over. After that, she poured a little homemade
apple cider vinegar in water for the last rinsing to take away the

terrible odor, swept it out and hobbled back to the bed sobbing
with excruciating pain. Her whole body was as hot as a
firecracker, and she throbbed from head to toe.

When Mama came home at dark, she washed her hands and came in
to see about Tacky. She laid her cool hand on Tacky's fevered
brow, and stood back in shock.

"Tacky, you're burning up with fever! I will get some
aspirin."

"Mama, it won't stay down. I already tried it."

"We must try again, Tacky, for your temperature is
dangerously high," Mama cried. So, Mama brought aspirin and some
water.

Tacky swallowed the aspirin, but vomited within a few
seconds. She grabbed the towel in Mama's hand to prevent making
another mess.

"Mama, I'm sorry to make more work for you, but the towel is
easier to clean than the floor." Tacky cried as she looked at
Mama with feverish eyes.

"Don't worry about the work, Child," Mama said, as she took
the towel, put it in a foot-tub of water, and brought a wash-pan
of water and a clean washcloth to sponge Tacky's face, neck, and
arms.

The cool water immediately sent Tacky into a chill. Mama had to
wrap her in blankets and quilts. She went to talk with Papa about
going for the doctor.

"Martha, we can't run to the doctor for every little
sickness. I'm sure she'll be better by morning. She's
probably just hot from working in the sun all day. Maybe I
kept her out too long."

"It's more than that, Robert," Mama declared.

"Well, we'll get a doctor in the morning if she isn't
better."

Tacky

All night Mama kept sponging Tacky's body to try to bring the temperature down. She tried giving a little toddy mixed with water, but it wouldn't stay down, either.

Early the next morning Papa came into Tacky's room, and said, "Tacky, I want you to get up and walk around and see if that helps."

Tacky looked at him with glazed eyes, then tried with all her might to get up and walk. When she put weight on her right foot, she screamed in pain and fell back across the bed, sobbing. Her right foot and leg were more painful than the boil. Her ankle was more swollen than before, and more red streaks now ran up and down her leg. Tacky's whole body racked with pain.

Papa said, "Tacky, you have just sprained your ankle from hobbling around, trying to protect the other leg. It can't be that bad."

Tacky had experienced sprained ankles before and knew that the pain torturing her was something new, but it wouldn't do any good trying to tell Papa how much she suffered. She was too sick to even talk. She lay helplessly on the bed with tears running from both eyes.

Mama looked at Papa with determination. "Robert, this child has to have a doctor. Her fever has been dangerously high all night, and she can't keep anything down to lower it. I want you to go or send someone after Dr. Brannon immediately."

"Let me try to get some aspirin down her." Papa said.

Mama handed him the aspirin bottle and a glass of water, then brought a pan to set beside the bed.

Papa took the aspirin and handed them to Tacky while he held the glass of water. "Here Tacky, take this and do your best to keep it down."

Wearily, Tacky obeyed. Seconds later, she threw up again.

Tacky

Papa went outside, saddled his horse, and rode to town for the doctor.

When Dr. Brannon saw Papa arrive, he knew something was wrong. Papa explained Tacky's problem.

"Leave your horse, here, Robert," Dr.Brannon said. "Ride in the car with me." He turned to a neighbor who worked in the flowerbed next door and said, "John, if we're not back within an hour, will you please take care of Mr. Mayberry's horse?"

"Sure, be glad to," he said.

When Dr. Brannon took Tacky's temperature, it was 105 degrees. He looked at her badly swollen ankle and the boil on her knee. He walked over to the window where Papa stood.

"Robert, this is much worse than a sprain. The boil needs lancing, but that doesn't worry me. I'll take care of that later. We need to get some x-rays of that ankle to see what's wrong."

"That will be quite expensive," Papa said.

"Yes, it will, but this is no ordinary problem. We must see what's causing the trouble."

Mama spread a quilt in the back seat of Dr. Brannon's car and added pillows for Tacky's head and leg. Dr. Brannon lifted her thin little body and carried her to the car.

Tacky tried not to cry, but by then, any movement tortured her.

Dr. Brannon placing her gently in the back seat, gave her an injection for the pain, and said, "Honey, I know every move is pure misery, but we we have to find out what is at the bottom of this."

The x-ray technician took several x-rays, but nothing showed up. He said, "These x-rays don't show anything, but if she were my child, I'd get her to a bone specialist immediately."

49

Dr. Brannon knew Papa would never agree to that. "It's probably tuberculosis of the bone or white swelling. I'll doctor for one, and if it's not better in a few days, I'll doctor for the other."

He picked up some strong antibiotics and pain medication, then gave Tacky an injection shot for pain and another for infection. When he brought her back home, he told Mama how to administer the medication.

By now, all Tacky wanted was to be left alone, and not be moved. Her pain grew more and more unbearable by the minute.

By the next afternoon, she was in such excruciating pain that all the neighbors heard her screaming. The medication for pain did not faze her. A great number of neighbors gathered to see if they could be of help. One went for the doctor. He gave her another injection for pain, but it had no effect.

Dr. Brannon said the swelling was so bad, it would be ready to lance in about three days. He promised to return and bring his instruments for that.

By midnight, Tacky's leg was as black as Papa's old hat and as big around as a five-gallon churn. Her screams had become low and almost lifeless. Another neighbor ran for the doctor.

When Dr. Brannon arrived he took one look and said, "Good Lord, I've never in my life seen anything like this." He took her and temperature and saw it was 107 degrees. "I can't believe this."

He shook the thermometer and and stuck it back under Tacky's hot tongue. She now lay lifeless from complete exhaustion and illness.

"Robert, we must get this child to the hospital immediately," Dr. Brannon said. "She's in a deathly condition."

Papa had a small insurance policy that covered treatment

in a hospital in East Birmingham. So, Mamma made a bed in the back
of the car, packed pillows around Tacky's black swollen leg and
started for the hospital, about 60 miles away, as fast as Dr.
Brannon thought it safe to drive. Every rough place brought
pitiful moans from Tacky's pale lips. About half way to the
hospital the car crossed over a railroad track, and the bumping
caused a shrieking scream, then, Tacky's small, fevered body went
completely limp.

Dr. Brannon pulled off the side of the road to see what
happened. "Good Lord, her leg's busted," he exclaimed. He packed
towels around it, as black and grey pus poured from a split in the
skin.

He got back in the car and drove like a maniac to the
hospital. Nurses rushed Tacky to x-ray upon her arrival at the
Woodlawn Hospital Emergency Room. Dr. Somerset, their best
orthopedic doctor was called in, took one look at the x-rays and
Tacky's leg, then spoke with Dr. Brannon and Papa.

*"Mr. Mayberry, this child must have emergency surgery
immediately. She has Osteomyelitis, an infection that begins
in the marrow of the bone, and eats holes through the bone,
leaving it like a honeycomb. That's is why her temperature is
so high, and the pain so severe."*

*"When the infection ate through the bone, it released the
infection into the flesh. When the flesh couldn't hold it anymore,
it broke open. I hate to tell you this, but very few people
survive this disease. We'll do everything in our power to save her
life. I'd appreciate it if you would start praying for me while I
operate."*

Dr. Brannon sat with Papa during the operation. "That
explains the uncontrollable pain," Dr. Brannon said. "The
infection was eating out the bone, and the pain medication can't
deaden bone."

"If it shows up on the x-rays here, why didn't it show up on the first ones we took?" Papa asked.

"It had not eaten completely through the bone in the first ones. And that made it harder to be seen." Dr. Brannon explained.

When Dr. Somerset came out of the operating room a few hours hours later, he said, "I split your child's leg in nineteen places. There was so much infection that I couldn't do much chiseling of the bone, until the infection drains out of the way. I don't think her frail little body will stand any more today. If she survives this, we will have to go back in there in a few days and chisel out the diseased bone."

They operated again on Saturday, allowing Papa to watch from a balcony. He was shocked when Dr. Somerset bored holes in Tacky's bone with a surgical brace and bit. He couldn't believe his eyes when the bit struck the marrow, it spurted like a geyser, sending pus as high as the ceiling. Then the doctors took surgical hammers and a chisel and chiseled out the diseased bone in the fibula, tibia, and the ankle joint.

Tacky's life hung by a thread. The infection remained bad, and her temperature stayed dangerously high.

A couple of weeks later Dr. Somerset called in eight orthopedic specialists to discuss amputation. He went to Tacky's room and sat beside her bed.

"Honey, I am sorry to have to tell you this, but to save your life, we will have to remove your leg." Tears welled up in his kind blue eyes, as he patted her shoulder and said, "We'll do everything possible for you, Honey."

Even though Tacky was deathly ill, Tacky felt sympathetic for him and wanted to ease his pain as much as possible. She put on a brave smile and squeezed his hand, saying weakily, "Don't worry, Dr. Somerset, I'm young. Maybe I'll just sprout a new leg."

Dr. Somerset stooped and hugged her and hurried from the room to hide his tears. He returned to the conference room to discuss the situation with the eight specialists. It broke his heart to consider removing the leg of that brave little eleven-year-old girl.

After much discussion, checking x-rays, reading charts and evaluating the pros and cons of the situation, four doctors voted to amputate, and four voted to try to save the leg.

Dr. Somerset prayed that the Lord would give him guidance and direction. *'Maybe I'll just sprout a new leg,'* kept playing through his mind. In the end, he couldn't amputate.

He drilled holes into Tacky's leg in eight places and inserted rubber tubes to drain the bone marrow. In the ankle, he drilled a hole through the joint, and cut a tube half into in it, allowing it to drain from both ends.

He chiseled out more of the ankle joint from the outside of the leg and more of the tibia in her shin. He chiseled and scraped out infected areas from the center of Tacky's foot to the knee.

When she was finally returned to her room, nurses placed a rubber sheet on the bed, and a rubber-covered pillow on a short table on the bed, to elevate Tacky's leg. Pus dripped out of the eight tubes constantly, as well as from both ends of the ankle tube.

Papa, a money-conscious man, worried about the cost and approached Dr. Somerset.

"Mr. Mayberry," the doctor said, "my prime concern is to save that child's life. I know that you, as a farmer, probably don't have much available cash, so I don't intend to charge you for this surgery. If you have a ham or pork shoulder you don't need, bring it to be sometime when you're back down this way."

Tacky

Mama remained at home, taking care of the farm and her family while worrying herself sick over Tacky. Papa didn't think they could afford to have both of them at the hospital.

When Tacky awoke after the surgery, the pain was so severe, she whispered to Dr. Somerset,"If I'd known it would still hurt this bad, I would've said, just leave it on."
He smiled and patted her shoulder tenderly,

"Honey, we decided not to remove your leg after all." Then he gave Tacky a shot for pain, and she drifted back to sleep.

Tacky remained ill for months. Pus dripped from all the tubes and formed little puddles on the rubber sheet. Nurses changed her bed several times a day—a torturous process—and the odor was so bad, no one could remain in the room for long.

When school began that fall, Tacky asked that someone bring her books to the hospital so she could keep up with her classes. Even though she was ill, she knew her sixth grade work would suffer if she got behind.

When she was able to return home for a few weeks, a classmate who passed her house each day would stop in the evenings to leave assignments and pick up the work Tacky did the next morning. The teacher and students were very cooperative.

She had six surgeries from the end of the fifth grade to the end of the sixth, but when she was home, the teacher came to her house and tested her on what the class learned while she was away. That made it possible for Tacky to pass the Sixth Grade.

Tacky

CHAPTER Eight

Each year, Tacky and her twin brothers always looked forward to the first week in August. During that time, a Revival always took place at the nearby Methodist Church, which was seven miles away. Papa said the mules needed to rest on Sundays, so the only time the family went to church was during a Revival or to a funeral.

Papa always tried to get his crops "laid-by" in time for the August Revival, which was a special week, and a time to pay tribute and reverence to God and have fun and fellowship with seldom-seen friends and neighbors. Almost everyone near and far attended the morning and evening services at that time.

The mules were hitched to the old wagon, with a quilt folded over two planks to create seats for Mama, Papa, and the older children. The tailgate was removed from the back, and a quilt folded across the bed for the younger ones to sit and let their feet dangle over the edge. Much of the time, the twins jumped off and ran behind the wagon.

The revival provided the highlight of the year. People, wearing their Sunday best, anticipated good preaching, singing, and fellowship.

Tacky

At the age of twelve, during the August Revival, Tacky
realized she was a sinner who needed the Savior. Tacky hadn't
thought of herself as a sinner before. The only really bad things
she could remember doing were stealing a handful of cotton and
cursing.   Every time she was tempted to do something against her
conscience, she saw rain pouring through a leaky roof, decaying
her body and soul. She was always careful to sort out words the
twins used before trying them herself, partly because she didn't
like being a slave to what the twins said.

"Everyone has sinned and come short of the glory of God,"
the preacher said. "We're like sheep who have gone astray, because
each of us want to go his own way."

Tacky thought, *I like to do things my own way. Maybe he's
talking about me after all.*

He said, "God sent a Shepherd who was willing to bear the
sins of the self-willed sheep. That Shepherd was Jesus, who was
also the Light of the World. Anyone who hasn't surrendered his
life to Jesus walks in darkness and will always do so until he
surrenders to the Savior."

Darkness scared Tacky. When she couldn't see what was
outside, she became afraid. She wanted a light to illuminate that
darkness.

The preacher said,"When Jesus spoke again to the people, He
said, "I am the light of the world. Whoever follows me will never
walk in darkness, but will have the light of life" (John 8:12.

Suddenly, Tacky wanted that Light in her life and felt
that unless she asked Jesus' forgiveness for all her disobedience
and sins, she'd walk in darkness the rest of her life. She
thought those deteriorating rains would break down her character
house.

Going to the altar on her crutches, she asked the preacher to
pray for Jesus to come into her life to forgive her and help her

to walk in His Light and avoid the evil, dark paths of life.   She prayed in her heart and the Preacher prayed aloud.

She felt an instant peace surround her like she had never felt before. Something warm and comforting came into her life, not an emotional spectacular entrance, but a great calm, a peace, a serenity, a feeling of joy, trust and security. Rodd and Todd went to the altar also, and Tacky hoped they felt the same joy and comforting peace that she felt.

After Christ came into Tacky's life she was no longer satisfied with just a once-a-year revival.   There was a little Baptist Church about a mile from her home, so she asked Mama if she could go to Sunday school and Preaching there.   It was close enough she could walk there on crutches.

Mama said,"Tacky, I don't mind your going to church close by, but since neither Papa nor I will be with you, I'd better not hear about you talking or acting bad in Church."

Tacky promised not to talk during services.   This wasn't hard to abide by, since she was such a shy little girl, but she was also a giggler. Everything seemed funny, especially in church. Snickering proved to be embarrassing, but she couldn't seem to control herself.

Every Sunday Morning, Tacky got up early, bathed, and dressed in her best clothes, then walked the mile on crutches to the little Baptist Church.   She tried hard to be quiet and reverent, but some of the older boys knew how to get her tickled, and never missed an opportunity.   They shook with laughter, until she giggled, then they cut their laughter off and were as reverent as the preacher himself, when adult heads turned in that direction.

One Sunday evening a visiting preacher, who was bald on top with just a little fuzz around the edges, was preaching. An older boy, sitting behind Tacky, tapped her on the shoulder and whispered,   "Gee, God sure was good to that preacher wasn't He?"

    "Why?" Tacky innocently asked.

    "He gave him one face, and cleaned off space for another,"
the young man said, then covered his mouth and shook with
laughter.

    The young man's remark completely embarrassed Tacky, and she
couldn't control her laughter; then, her face turned red from
shame and humiliation. She was so ashamed, but just couldn't help
it; therefore, she was always in trouble both at church and at
home. Many times Papa sent her and Todd to bed without their
supper for laughing at the supper table. Rodd always appeared
solemn when Papa looked up at the sound of muffled laughter, but
Tacky and Todd were never able to stop and put on a solemn
expression.

    Even though Tacky was crippled and walked on crutches, she
still thought she could do anything the twins did. Some narrow
rails on the bridge that crossed the creek near their home
afforded the twins much enjoyment. The twins climbed on them and
balanced themselves by holding their arms out as they walked
across.

    Tacky thought she had to learn how to do that with crutches.
It took two weeks of attempts before she could stand up balanced
on one foot. Then she would put her crutches on the narrow rail
and walk sideways for a step or two, only to lose her balance and
jump down on one foot.

    She kept trying until she managed to walk across the rail
using her crutches. Often, she stood on one foot while she flailed
the air with her crutches, only to lose her balance and fall off.
The twins cheered when she made it across the creek without
jumping off. She liked their approval and would do almost anything
to gain it.

Tacky

When there was a large snowfall, she begged to go out and
play in it like the twins. At first Papa said no, but she kept
begging until he took a tow sack that once held cottonseed meal
and showed her how to wrap it tightly around her crippled foot,
then tie it with strips torn from an old garment to keep her leg
warm.

It was difficult raising her crutches high enough to get
them out of the snow, but she refused to give up. She stretched
them out in front of her and swung her small, scrawny body as far
forward as she could. It was important for her to do the things
she set out to do, because the twins teased her if she failed.
Besides, she felt embarrassed in front of her friends if she
couldn't perform up to their expectations. Tacky thought the twins
were just doing it to make her life difficult, but later in life,
she realized they helped her adjust to her afflictions.

Even though she continued to have more surgeries, she did her
best to live as normal a life as possible and not burden anyone.
She did her share of work around the house, washing dishes and
making beds. In fact, Tacky learned how to turn on her good foot
and make beds very quickly.

Tacky

Chapter Nine

Tacky sat by the window with tears trickling down her
freckled face, as she had each morning for the past week and
a half, when the school bus passed. She thought, *If Frisk
were here, he'd pat my shoulder, and say, Tacky, dry those tears,
before you add more rusty spots.*

She already had plenty of freckles on her face, and now it
was so swollen from crying that even her blue eyes looked faded.
She wanted to be on that school bus more than anything in her
twelve years of life.

She had begged and pleaded with Papa to let her go to
school, but he refused her.

"Now, Tacky, there is just no way you can go to school.
There are books and school supplies to buy, tuition to pay, and
look what I'm already payin' in doctor and hospital bills.
Besides, you're already good at reading, writing, and arithmetic.
What more education do you need? You will probably never do more
than cook, keep house, and raise a family."

"But Papa, even then, I need more than a sixth grade
education. Besides, I want to be able to get a job and pay my own

expenses, and repay you for all you've spent on me. Dr. Somerset told you I would never be able to make a field hand again."

"Tacky, there's no use keepin' on about this. Your school days are over. and you might as well forget about it!"

Tacky went to her room in tears, but she never forgot about school. She prayed day and night that something would happen to change Papa's mind. Each day as she saw the bus pass, she prayed.

That morning, she wiped her eyes, bowed her head and whispered: "Dear God, I'm so mixed up. I believe You really want me to go to school. I believe my strong desire comes from You, but nothing seems to come of it. Papa doesn't seem to budge in any way. I can't do it without Your help, but please change Papa's mind. School has been going on for almost two weeks, and I am gettin' farther and farther behind. Please God, Please help me find a way to get an education."

A peace seemed to enter Tacky's heart, and she whispered, "Thank You, Lord!" She picked up her crutches, went to the back porch where the water bucket and a wash pan sat on a shelf. She dipped fresh cool water into the wash pan and washed her swollen face and eyes, and went back to her room, picked up her Bible and read some.

She heard a truck drive up, and pulled aside her curtains made of fertilizer sacks and saw Uncle Ted, Papa's younger brother climbing out of his pick-up truck. Excitedly she picked up her crutches and hurried to the door to greet him.

"Hi Tacky, I thought you'd be in school," Uncle Ted remarked.

"Papa won't let me go." Tacky explained.

"Why, are you not strong enough yet?"

"Oh, it isn't that. I am better and could go now, but Papa says he doesn't have the money." Tacky sadly answered.

Tacky

"Tacky, go to your room, I'm sure Ted didn't come to listen to your problems," Papa snapped. He had heard all he wanted to hear about school.

Tacky, obediently went to her room, picked up some embroidery, trying to think of something besides school. But try as she might, her intense longing kept returning.

After a short visit with Papa, Uncle Ted knocked on Tacky's door, and said, "Tacky, it's time for me to go, but since you aren't in school, why don't you go home with me for a few days?"

Tacky grabbed her crutches and hurried to the living room, "Oh Papa, Uncle Ted wants me to go home with him. May I?"

"Tacky, that would be too much trouble for Ted. He'd have to make another trip to bring you back and that costs money, you know," Papa replied.

"Oh, I don't mind that, Robert. The family will be thrilled with a visit from Tacky, and I'm sure it'd do her good, too." Uncle Ted hurriedly replied.

"Well, if it isn't too much trouble. She's no good in the field anymore. If Martha doesn't need her help, I guess it'll be all right."

Tacky hurried to the kitchen.."Oh Mama, Uncle Ted's here, and has asked me to come home with him. Papa said I could if you don't need me to help you."

Mama looked at Tacky's eyes, still red from crying, and thought *maybe this is what she needs to get her mind off school. She* finished the crowfoot design on a beautiful cake of freshly churned butter, set it in the safe, put an arm around Tacky's shoulder."Tacky, honey, I think a change is just what you need. I'll make out fine here." She dried her hands on a fertilizer sack towel and went to the living room, hugged Uncle Ted and invited him to stay for lunch.

Uncle Ted smiled and his eyes twinkled as he said. "Martha, I'd love to sit down to one of your delicious meals, but Eula doesn't even know where I sneaked off to. She'll have the County Sheriff out huntin' me if I don't return soon."

Tacky loved seeing the twinkle in Uncle Ted's eyes, and the laugh lines around his mouth. They always warmed her heart. He seemed to be filled with warmth and mischief all at the same time.

"I'll get my things." She said and rushed out. She put a few clothes and her pajamas in a paper bag, then gathered supplies for doctoring and dressing her leg and hurried out. She could hardly wait to get started on this exciting journey.

She hugged Mama, "Thanks for lettin' me go."

Uncle Ted helped her into the old truck, placing her clothes and leg dressings beside her and whistling a cheery tune. A moment later, he climbed into the truck, and they drove off.

As soon as they were out on the road, he looked at Tacky and asked, "Do you really want to go to school?"

"Do I? Oh Uncle Ted! I've never wanted anything in my whole life, but Papa's put out a lot of money because of my surgeries, and he'd never pay another penny for schoolin'."

"Would you be willing to work to pay your way through?"

"OH, I'd be willin' to do anything decent if I could make enough to pay my expenses, but what can I do on crutches to earn that much?"

"I don't know, but tomorrow I'm going to talk with the Principal at School and see." His merry eyes were filled with a determined glint, something Tacky recognized from Mama's eyes.

As they drove into the yard, Aunt Eula stepped onto the porch. "Goodness, Ted, I didn't know where you'd run off to," she scolded.

"I know," Uncle Ted said, as he gave her a bear hug and kissed her cheek. "I was goin' to the hayfield, when I got a

strong urge to go over to Robert's for a little visit. I thought
I'd be back by the time I came back to tell you."

Aunt Eula hugged Tacky and almost didn't hear Uncle Ted's
words. "Tacky, it's so good to see you, but I thought you'd be in
school."

"It's a long story, Aunt Eula. Uncle Ted will explain it
to you." She felt tears gathering in her eyes. Tacky hated showing
her emotions, but when the subject of school came up, she
couldn't hide them.

There may be a way yet. Uncle Ted's goin' to see tomorrow.
She brightened as she remembered their conversation.

Aunt Eula looked puzzled at Uncle Ted, then looked back at
Tacky's tear-swollen eyes, "Come this way Dear, we'll put your
things in this room, which you can claim as your very own until
the girls get in from school. Then all three of you can share it.
Now let's have some lunch."

When the school bus stopped, Tacky hurried out to meet Ida
and Tillie.

"Tell me about school," Tacky said breathlessly. Are there
many goin'? Is the work hard? Are the teachers good to you?"

"Hey, wait a minute!" Ida raised her hand in protest.

"I've never heard so many questions about school."
Tillie laughed, "And come to think about it, just why aren't you
in school?" She asked, with wonderment in her eyes.

"It costs too much." Tacky said.

"Costs too much! Who ever heard? I sure wish it cost too
much for us to go. Ida complained.

"My six surgeries in the last fifteen months cost Papa so
much that he doesn't want to waste money on schoolin',"
Tacky explained. "But Uncle Ted is goin' to talk with the
Principal tomorrow, to see if there is anyway I can work to
pay my expenses," her eyes dancing with excitement.

"I know several people who work in different areas of the school," Ida said. "I never thought about it before, but maybe they're payin' their expenses, too."

Before going to sleep that night, Tacky prayed fervently that God would help Uncle Ted work something out--and that Papa would allow her to go.

Tacky heard Tillie whisper sleepily, "I wish I wanted to go to school that badly."

Tacky tossed and turned all night, too excited to sleep. For the first time since school began, she felt encouraged that something might allow her to attend.

The following morning. Uncle Ted drove Ida and Tillie to school and went to the office to talk with Mr. Barefoot, the principal.

That day, Tacky made dozens of trips to the window and back.

Aunt Eula said, "Child, you're wearin' yourself out. I was always told, 'A watched pot never boils.'" She laughed.

"In the Bible, in Matthew 21:22, it says, 'All things whatsoever ye shall ask in prayer believing, ye shall receive.' Do you think that might include goin' to school?"

After talking the situation over with Uncle Ted the previous night, Aunt Eula feared raising Tacky's hopes.

She put her arm around the child and said,"Tacky, don't get your hopes up too much....God doesn't always answer our prayers just the way we want them answered. If He did, you wouldn't be having all this trouble with your leg. We must trust Him, and realize that in the long run, He will work out what is best for us. But it may not be just the way we want it. Do you understand?" She asked tenderly.

"I think so. I don't want anything that's contrary to God's Will. But I need an education so I won't always be a burden to my parents or others. I'll love and praise God even if He sees it differently, but I just know He'll make a way for me to go back to school!" She spoke as if it were a fact.

A worried look came to Aunt Eula's eyes. "I surely hope so, Honey." Finally, Tacky heard the old truck rattling down the road. Grabbing her crutches, she rushed outside to meet Uncle Ted.

"Oh, Uncle Ted, what job did I get?"

Uncle Ted slowly climbed out of the truck, put his arm around Tacky, and replied.."Tacky, let us go inside and sit down with a cup of coffee and I'll tell you all about my trip."

Aunt Eula heard his reply and poured coffee as the pair came into the kitchen. She gave Tacky a cup of hot chocolate, and they all sat around the kitchen table.

"There's a National Youth Association that pays five cents an hour, for different chores done around the school," Uncle Ted explained, "to youth who need assistance. But since school's been going on almost two weeks, all the good jobs are already taken. The only job left is scrubbin' lavatories, toilet seats, and bad words off the toilet walls."

"Oh, I don't mind the hard, dirty work, if I can make enough to pay all my expenses," Tacky said. I need to make enough to buy books, paper, pencils, tuition, and everything. Papa wouldn't let me go any other way!"

"I know that, and I talked with Mr. Barefoot about it, but he assured me there's plenty of work. In fact, he called it an unending task!" Uncle Ted laughed.

"Oh, Uncle Ted! I love you!" Tacky said as she rushed over and hugged his neck. "Will you please take me home and talk Papa into lettin' me go?"

"What's your hurry?" When he saw her so excited, his eyes sparkled like the sky on a cold winter's night.

"There'll be so many things to get ready, and I don't want to miss the bus in the mornin'."

Tacky

Tacky was bubbling over. She hugged Aunt Eula and thanked her for a lovely visit, and promised to come back as soon as she could.

Uncle Ted helped her carry her things out to the old truck, and to Tacky, the whole world looked bright and lovely on that bright September day in 1937.

When Uncle Ted helped her out of the truck, she rushed inside shouting, "Oh, Papa, Mama, Uncle Ted has some fantastic news to tell you. He has fixed it where I can go to school!"

"Tacky, I thoughtI told you to forget school," Papa scolded in disgust. "I didn't know you were going down there to fuss about school, I have told you over and over again that we can't afford it! And I don't know what it is goin' to take to get that across to you!"

"I know, Papa, but this way it won't cost you anything."

"Tacky, you know we don't accept charity!" Papa raised his eyebrows in complete disgust.

"Oh, it isn't charity, Papa. Uncle Ted, please explain it to Papa."

Uncle Ted smiled and turned to Papa. He explained in full detail all about NYA work, how the association was formed especially for those who couldn't attend without assistance. It wouldn't be charity, because it involved hard, dirty work the school would have to pay to have done, anyway.

"But she couldn't make enough to pay ALL her expenses that way," Papa reasoned.

"I questioned that too,but Mr. Barefoot assured me that she could!"

"Oh, Papa, please let me try it. I promise I'll do a good job. Those toilets and lavatories will be the cleanest in the whole county! You'll never have to be ashamed of me for not doin' my work right! Please say yes, Papa, Please!"

"It would be a great opportunity for Tacky, and you wouldn't have anything to lose, Robert, since she is unable to work in the field, anyway," Uncle Ted reasoned.

"Well, maybe not, as long as you're sure I won't be out any expenses. I guess she can try it, but the first time I have to pay for anything, it's over. Do you understand that, Tacky?"

"Oh, yes, Papa. Thank you! Thank you!" Tacky cried, fiercely hugging his neck.

Mama had sat quietly listening with tears in her eyes. She got up and went to Uncle Ted, hugged him and thanked him for all his trouble.

"It was my pleasure, Martha." He assured her.

Tacky put her arms around his neck and whispered, "Uncle Ted, I'll never forget all you've done for me, and one day I'll make you proud of me."

"I'm already proud of you, Tacky!" He said as he squeezed her and stooped down to kiss her forehead.

Mama and Tacky took some picksack ducking and cut out a book bag with a shoulder strap to go across Tacky's neck and shoulder so her hands would be free to use the crutches. Tacky sewed it together and hunted up the books Rodd had started in the seventh grade with several years before. "Maybe I can exchange these for what I need," she said.

She washed her hair, pressed her best skirt and blouse, polished her high-top shoes, shined her brace, and dusted and polished her crutches. She wanted everything to look its best. After all, she had never been to high school before and wanted to be accepted from the start.

CHAPTER TEN

Tacky was out on the road bright and early Friday Morning waiting for the school bus. She knew the driver would not be looking for her and wanted to be sure she didn't get left. She slung the booksack over her shoulder with the heavy books, so her hands would be free to use her crutches. The bus steps were high, so it took several attempts to get up with her frail body and heavy books. She blushed with embarrassment when the bus driver got up to help her just as she made it up by herself.

Upon arriving at school, she went to the principal's office to get a list of her duties and directions to her classes. The people were kind and helpful, but Tacky felt like a misplaced ant among such efficient people.

One of her greatest desires was to do well in her schoolwork and job, so Papa and Uncle Ted would be proud of her. She knew Papa would never say anything, but she'd know, and that was important. He spent a lot of money on her already. She wanted to be able to repay him somehow. Since she couldn't do field work anymore, she needed an education to find a job later in life. She couldn't afford to lose the opportunity.

As she went from class to class, Tacky was relieved to find she could use most of the books, and there were only a few items she needed to purchase. Mama sold butter and eggs to the peddler and let her have the money to buy those things. Tacky carefully wrote down every penny she spent in a little notebook, so she could repay Mama when she drew her first paycheck.

The principal told Tacky she could take her study period, recess, and lunch periods for her scrubbing tasks.

When her first study period came, she went to the supply room, got the cleaning items she needed, and went to the toilets. First, she swept the cob-webs from the walls and ceiling and picked up paper off the floor. Some paper trailed out the door.

Then she scrubbed down the walls until all the bad words and love notes were erased. After scrubbing the toilet seats, she swept the dirt floors, rinsed everything and stood back amazed at how different the room was. She felt proud but exhausted. It hadn't occurred to her how weak she was.

She smiled at a job well done. "One down and umpteen to go. I'll get more my next free period."

By the time school ended for the day, Tacky was exhausted, but she didn't want anyone to know. Arriving home, she ate freshly baked tea cakes and drank a glass of milk Mama prepared, knowing Tacky would be tired. Tacky liked taking two tea cakes, placing a slice of butter between them, and eating them as a sandwich. That tasted good with cool milk.

Mama took time from her busy schedule to sit with Tacky while she ate and listen to her talk about her day at school. Tacky knew how deeply Mama cared, so she made sure she told her how kind and helpful the people at school were. She elaborated on the principal's kindness and made her work sound simple. Even though she felt drained, Tacky took her books to her room to study for the coming day's lessons.

Tacky

Soon after Tacky started working at school, her classmates and teachers commented on how clean the toilets and the drinking fountains looked. Some said they were the cleanest in the county. Tacky beamed with pride. She wanted to do the best job possible.

Her first year of high school was difficult. Tacky was absent for six more weeks for surgery. Changing classes was new to her, and her heavy book bag cut into her shoulder. Tom, a classmate, offered to carry her books for her, but Tacky didn't want to be a burden to anyone and said, "Tom, that's sweet, and I appreciate it, but I need to build up my weak muscles. This is one way to do that."

The principal called Tacky to his office just before school ended one day. Tacky wondered what he wanted.

"Have a seat, Tacky," Mr. Barefoot said. "I want to talk to you about your work."

Fear rose in her throat. "Oh, Mr. Barefoot, is something wrong with it?"

"Goodnes, no. I have never seen such a perfect job, nor such a good attitude. People remark about the perfection of your schoolwork and your cleaning. It's just that I don't feel you're strong enough to do that kind of thing."

Fear filled her. "Oh Mr. Barefoot, I can do it. Please don't take it away from me. I can't go to school without this job."

"I don't want you to stop work. There's a girl working in the library who'll graduate in a couple of weeks, and I want you to work with her during one of your class periods until school is over. Once you learn the job, you can work in the library next year. It'll be easier for you."

Tacky sighed in relief. "Thank you, Mr. Barefoot. I appreciate that."

She continued cleaning but took one period a day to learn how to repair and mend books and how to check them in and out for the

students. She could hardly wait until the coming year. There were
some books she would love to read, but school was almost over, and
she had too much studying for exams to begin reading them now.

When School began again in the fall, Tacky had saved enough
money from her previous year's work to repay Mama all the money
she borrowed and her tuition. She sold her seventh-grade books and
was able to buy books for the eighth grade.

Tacky was excited to begin her school year without using
credit. She had to be very careful about buying pencils,
notebooks, and paper though, because her savings would soon be
exhausted. All her money went for school supplies. She never
considered buying something for herself.

As Tacky replaced backs on books and repaired torn, damaged
pages, she thanked God for Mr. Barefoot's concern in giving her a
better job. She liked working in the Library, partly because it
gave her the chance to become familiar with many books.

She began checking out books to read at home. In fact, she
talked so much about *Pilgrim's Progress*, her family became
interested and wanted her to read it to them.

Soon, reading by lamplight around the fire became the
family's pastime. Papa settled comfortably in his special rocker
beside the window near the fire. Mama moved her rocker near to
the old oil lamp so she could patch quilts while Tacky read. Rodd
and Todd stretched out on the floor before the fire.

Tacky placed a chair with a pillow on it for her crippled
leg, because it was swelling, and the doctors said to elevate it
whenever she could.

Tacky was so excited to be reading aloud that her eyes
swooped across the pages like a barn swallow across a hayfield.
The characters came alive and became her favorite people. Mrs.
Wiggs In the *Cabbage Patch*, Louisa Mae Alcott's, *Little Women*,
Little Men, and *Jo's Boys*, and *In His Steps*, all seemed so real to

her. She felt like joining the other Christians who asked, "What would Jesus do?" in all circumstance before deciding, just like in the book *In His Steps.*

The family enjoyed those books, but the Zane Gray novels became favorites of Papa and the twins. They enjoyed Westerns. Soon, Papa was borrowing Zane Gray Books from anyone he could. He finally gave in and spent some of his own money to buy a few copies and subscribed to *Ranch Romance Magazine,* a monthly magazine. Tacky was astounded that Papa found something he enjoyed so much.

Even though she knew her family liked to hear her read to them, she never did until she finished all her homework. That caused a commotion with the twins more than once.

One day, Todd came in from the mailbox, all excited. "Tacky, *Ranch Romance* just came in! I can't wait to hear the continued story."

"I can't read it right now, Todd. I have homework to do; besides, the rest of the family will want to hear it tonight."

"Ah, come on Sis. Just read a little to see if Tom got his hands and feet untied and got himself out of that old, abandoned shack."

"No, Todd. Run along. I have to study. I'll read it tonight."

Grumbling, he left the room. After Tacky finished her homework, she thumbed through the magazine. Todd came in at that moment and thought she was reading it without him.

Grabbing it from her, he shouted, "Yeah, you had homework and couldn't read it to me. As soon as I was out of sight, you picked up this magazine to finish the story!"

"I haven't read a word of it, I just finished my homework and picked up this magazine to glance through it."

"That's what you say!" Todd said as he slapped her.

Tacky hopped up on one foot and tried to get out of his way, but he was ready for her. She shouted at him, trying to make him listen, only he shouted the louder.

Rodd finally walked in. "What's going on in here?" He held Todd's shoulder.

"She's reading the story!" Todd shouted. "She doesn't intend to read it to us!"

"That's not so!" Tacky said. "I haven't even turned to that story. I had just finished studying and picked up the magazine to look through it when Todd came in."

Rodd shoved Todd into a chair and said, "Shame on you for pickin' on your little, crippled sister!"

Tacky's jaw dropped in amazement. Usually, the twins ganged up on her. When that happened, her being young and crippled didn't seem to matter.

Tacky

CHAPTER ELEVEN

The next five years Tacky was out of school every year
for more surgery. At age sixteen, Tacky was in the hospital for
more leg surgery, but her tonsils and adenoids were so enlarged,
she couldn't swallow anything except soft food or liquids, and she
couldn't breathe through her nose.

The neighbors worked with a state social worker and had Tacky
placed in the State Crippled Children's Clinic in Birmingham, so
Papa wouldn't lose his farm due to medical debts.

Dr. Conwell, the Orthopedic Surgeon called in an Ear, Nose,
and Throat doctor to look at Tacky's condition, which he wanted
cleared up before he performed another operation on her leg. The
infection in that part of her body drained her of her body's
healing power. The specialist said Tacky's tonsils and adenoids
had to be removed.

The west wing of South Highland Hospital was reserved for the
State Crippled Children's Clinic patients. Most were osteo
patients who had to stay after surgery for many months. Their
parents frequently lived so far away and were so poor, they
couldn't visit their children very often.

Tacky

    The kids became an extended family. Those on crutches or in
wheel chairs gathered in the rooms of patients that were bedfast,
and played dominoes, assembled puzzles, and passed the time
happily. They saved sugar packets and lemon slices from their
meal trays and made lemonade to serve when they were together.

    Miss Lambert, their favorite nurse, had a boyfriend called
JD, who heard her talk about the patients on the west wing so much
that he came in early when he had a date with her. He visited the
kids while Miss Lambert prepared to leave. The kids loved having
someone new to talk to and looked forward to his visits.

    JD had a new car with a musical horn. Miss Lambert had to be
in before midnight, so he would bring her back to the dormitory on
time, then drove up the mountain behind the hospital. At the
stroke of midnight, he played *Mary Had a Little Lamb* or *Yankee
Doodle*. That was his good-night message to the west-wing kids, and
they looked forward to it.

    One night he stopped the musical medley in the middle of the
tune. The kids felt certain the cops were the reason, because JD
had been playing for them for many nights. After explaining why he
was doing it, he received only a warning, but he had to stop
making so much noise after that. He played the tune on special
occasions afterward, but the kids missed hearing him. It was fun
to stay awake to hear the musical horn.

    They were so accustomed to surgery, they kidded each other,
saying, "After your surgery tomorrow, we'll watch for you to be
brought out of the basement door covered with a sheet and placed
in a hearse."

    They loved to gather in a patient's room just as he or she was
recovering from anesthetic, usually sodium pentathol. Then they
asked ridiculous questions just to hear the person give silly
answers; later, they kidded them mercilessly about it.

    They teased Tacky about a boy named Elmo.

Tacky

"We'll make you ask him to hold your hand as you come to," they said.

She was determined that wouldn't happen. The last thing she remembered as she was being anesthetized for her tonsillectomy was, "*I won't call for Elmo to hold my hand.*"

When she was returned to her room, a nurse stayed to check her vital signs, but she soon left.

Carl slipped in. "Tacky, don't you want Elmo to come hold your hand?" He asked.

Tacky only grunted.

"It would make you feel better and help your throat to stop hurting, Carl said convincingly. "Why don't you call him?"

Tacky whispered, "Elmo...."

"Louder, Tacky. He can't hear you. Call him to come hold your hand."

Tacky said a little louder, "Elmo, come hold my hand."

"Elmo! Come hold my hand! Please, Elmo." Then she gurgled, and blood ran from her lips.

Frightened, Carl rang for the nurse.

They rushed Tacky back into surgery to stop the bleeding. That was the last time any of the kids were allowed into Tacky's room for several days.

Three days later, Tacky told the nurse.."*Feel underneath my ears, I believe I am taking the mumps.*"

"*Tacky, you can have more wrong with you than anyone I have ever seen, but there's no way you can be taking the mumps as long as you have been in this hospital.*"

"*Maybe not, but it sure feels like it,*" Tacky said.

"That's a natural feeling after all you went through, with the tonsillectomy, plus having to go back to surgery because of your hollering. Just settle down and in a few days you'll feel better."

Tacky

Tacky wasn't convinced that she wasn't taking the mumps so,
that afternoon when the Intern made his rounds she asked him to
check. After feeling underneath her ears, and the neck glands, he
said, "Tacky, it seems impossible for you to take the mumps as
long as you have been in the hospital and haven't been exposed to
any, but it sure feels as though you might be. It's suspicious
enough to put you in isolation, for we sure don't want a mump
epidemic up here."

The Intern went to the desk to see if a private room was
available. He quickly ordered Tacky sent there until a diagnosis
could be made.

Nurses moved Tacky's bed beside the door in the new room, so
anything she needed could be handed to her without anyone having
to enter the room There was a wardrobe on the wall at the foot of
the bed with a full-length mirror.

The following morning after a restless night, Tacky looked at
herself in the mirror and was shocked at how big her face and jaws
were. She looked like one of Papa's hogs ready for slaughter.
When she tried to laugh at her image, her jaw cramped.

Miss Lambert cracked the door to check on Tacky. "Oh, my
goodness! You really do have the mumps, and a good case, don't
you? I'm sorry I laughed at you. I thought it was impossible. I
wonder who brought them to you?"

Miss Lambert was telling JD that night about Tacky's mumps.
"Oh, my goodness," he said. "I'll bet I brought them to her."
"You? How in the world could you have done that? You don't
have them."

"No, but I was around someone a week or two ago, who did.
Tacky's throat was just being operated on. Maybe that made it
easy for the bug to germinate in her."

Tacky soon recuperated from her surgery and mumps. Dr.
Conwell operated on her leg, removing more bone, and putting

more rubber drainage tubes in. She had to stay in bed with
her leg elevated on a pillow and a heat tent over it.

One week after the surgery, Dr. Conwell came in to see the
little girl sharing Tacky's room, who he operated on that morning,
only to find Tacky up on one elbow, vomiting.

"What's wrong,Tacky?" He came to her bed. As soon as Tacky
could stop vomiting long enough, she fell back on her pillow and
Dr. Conwell wet a washcloth in ice water and sponged her face.

"What happened, Honey?" He asked tenderly.

"A pain like a knife sticking in the middle of my stomach
ripped over to my right side, and I became sick. I had to vomit."

He pulled down the cover, placed his hand on her stomach,
then pressed. She screamed in pain, and he immediately called a
nurse.

"Get a lab technician in here immediately," he said. Tacky,
Honey, how can we contact your parents?"

"You can't. They lived seven miles from town. There aren't
any phones, not even electricity." She groaned in pain.

"We have to perform emergency surgery on you, and we can't
wait for them to get here. On the other hand, they can sue us if
we don't get word to them before we operate. Your appendix has to
come out. Who can we call?"

"Uncle Bill Puckett, Mama's brother-in-law. He works for
Hall's Store in Collinsville. He'll let them know."

"Is it just called Hall's Store?"

"I believe it's Hall's Clothing Store." She clutched her
side.

"Miss Lambert, please call Bill Puckett at Hall's Clothing
Store in Collinsville. When you get him, I need to speak with him"

She left just as the lab technician came in. A moment later,
her voice came over the intercom. "Dr. Conwell? Mr. Puckett's on
the line."

Dr. Conwell ran to the phone. "This is Dr. Conwell at South Highland Hospital in Birmingham. Tacky, your niece, has acute appendicitis. We must operate immediately. Can you get word to her parents? I can't wait for them to come here, and someone must tell them."

"I'll go on my lunch hour."

Tacky's white blood cell count rose rapidly. Dr. Conwell ordered a gurney to take her to the operating room. He gave her an injection for the pain, then rushed down to speak with the doctor who would perform the surgery.

When the gurney arrived, Miss Lambert and the OR nurse helped Tacky on it. The pain was terrible when she moved.

When the elevator door opened for them to get on, there was Papa waiting to get off. Even though Tacky was seriously ill, she recognized him.

"How did you get here so quick?" The nurse asked.

"Didn't seem quick to me. I left before eight this morning, and it's now noon. What's wrong with you, Tacky? Where are you going?"

Miss Lambert stepped up. "Mr. Mayberry, Dr. Conwell has been trying to locate you. He'll be glad you're here. Just ride the elevator with us, and I'll get him when we're downstairs."

"What's wrong?" Papa realized Tacky was very ill. "I thought she was doing fine since her leg surgery. She wrote she was OK,but I felt worried about her and decided to come down."

"She was fine until an hour or two ago. Dr. Conwell will explain it to you." Miss Lambert patted his shoulder as they reached the operating room floor, and the gurney rolled through the open elevator doors. "Just wait in the waiting room across the hall, and Dr. Conwell will see you shortly."

Shocked, wondering what was going on, Papa paced the hall until Dr. Conwell arrived.

Tacky

Shaking Papa's hand, Dr. Conwell said, "Mr. Mayberry, I'm
sorry to have to give you more bad news. It seems your poor child
has more things happen to her than anyone we know. She has acute
appendicitis, but, thank the Lord, she's in a hospital where we
can operate quickly. Her appendix is ready to rupture, if it
hasn't already, and it's less than two hours since her first pain.
I'm glad you're here in time for the surgery.

"Have a seat in the waiting room. I'll keep you posted." Dr.
Conwell left the room.

Papa sat there thinking of all that happened to Tacky. Over
the past two-and-a-half years, she had eight leg surgeries,
then she had her tonsils and adenoids removed, then caught the
mumps. Two weeks after her most-recent leg surgery, she had
appendicitis.

"Why? he wondered."Why Tacky? She tries so hard to do
everything right." He walked to the window to cover up his
unusual emotional outburst.

Tacky soon recovered and returned home and to school, where
she caught up on the work she missed while she was in the
hospital.

War broke out with Germany and Japan. The twins enlisted in
the army. Todd was sent to the Philippines, while Rodd went to
Germany. Several years earlier Bill joined the Civilian
Conservation Corps, and transferred from there into the Army.

Tacky was in the hospital for three months during her senior
year of high school. One day Dr. Conwell came in and sat on the
edge of her bed. "Now that you'll be graduating, what do
you plan to do?"

"Go into nurse's training."

"Honey, I've been hoping all these years you wouldn't do
that. "Your leg will never be strong enough."

"I've always wanted to help sick people."

"I know, I've seen you doing it for years, even when you were in worse shape than some of the patients. You'd make an excellent nurse, someone I'd be proud to work with, but, you will never be physically strong enough to be on your feet all day."

"Good Secretaries are always in demand. Why not attend business college and train as a secretary?"

"If God wants me to be a nurse, He'll give me the strength." Although disappointed, she wasn't discouraged. There were other fields where God might need her.

When Tacky returned to school, she took tests and passed all the work she missed. When she was elected valedictorian of her class, she was honored with a Daughters of the American Revolution award, and won a scholarship to a business college in Birmingham. She felt certain God was still watching out for her.

As she thought back over her life and prepared her speech for graduation, she realized that what seemed a great tragedy in her life had become a tremendous blessing.

Had she not been crippled, she would've been able to work in the fields and never would've gotten past the sixth grade. Despite having twelve operations on her leg, a tonsillectomy, adenoidectomy and appendectomy between the fifth and twelfth grades, she also had the opportunity for more education.

She thought of the long hard hours of work at five cents an hour, and how she learned thrift by having to pay her school expenses on a small income. Papa taught her not to expect a handout and to work for what she wanted. She was thankful to God, Uncle Ted, and Papa.

Tacky truly believed Romans 8:28, where Paul said, "And we know that all things work together for good to them that love God, to them who are the called according to His purpose."

She felt God had taken her tragedy and turned it into the greatest blessing she could've had.

Thinking about all that, she wrote a poem.

THANK GOD FOR OUR BLESSINGS

*If we thank God for our blessings every
single day,
We'll be surprised how our blessings grow,
and our troubles fade away.
For He's always waiting, eager to bless,
And it's only when we go our way that
things become a mess.
We have a tendency to rush through life,
Bemoaning all the struggle and strife,
But do we ever take time to stop and
analyze
That many of our troubles come from
being unwise?
God says ask, and He'll give us wisdom for
the day,
When we let Him lead, life becomes easier
along the way.
He's always as close as the outstretched
hand,
And to help us through life is in His plan,
But, He can only bless to the extent
that we trust and believe.
When we trust Him with all our heart, His
blessings we receive.*

Tacky was anxious to prepare for her trip to Birmingham to finish her education. She couldn't wait to find a job and repay Papa for all he spent on her.

There was another reason to hurry with her plans, too. She became quite interested in a nearby country boy, who didn't want

Tacky

her to attend business college. He feared she might find someone
else, so he wanted them to marry right away. Tacky explained she
had obligations to fulfill before she would be free to marry
anyone.

"Cranston, if I don't love you enough to wait for you, you'll
be better off without me, anyway," She said.

"I will never be better off without you, Tacky. I love
you. You mean more to me than anyone in the world, and
I want us to have a life together." He put his arm around her and
held her against his big, strong body.

"I know you do, and I love you, too. I want to marry you,
too, but I've been planning all these years to repay Papa. I won't
let anything stop that."

"We could repay him together."

"No. This is my responsibility. Besides, I have a
scholarship, and it won't take long. I'll study hard and finish my
secretarial course in record time."

She gently pulled herself away. "Cran, you'll be proud of me
when I finish school and get a good job to help with our expenses
if we get married."

"Don't say if, say when." I love you so much,life would be
meaningless without you. I'll be glad to make the living myself,
so you won't have to work."

"I know, and I appreciate that, but I want to be able to
help. I never want to be a handicap to anyone."

"I know. I guess that is one thing that makes me love you so
much is how you always think of others first. I'll wait if you
insist, but I want so much to make you my wife. Then we could be
together, and I could make things easier for you."

"I love and appreciate you for that. I'll work hard to finish
my studies fast and repay my debts, then we can begin our life
together without any handicap."

Tacky

Tacky

CHAPTER TWELVE

After graduation, Tacky mended, washed, and ironed all her
best clothes and packed them in two old, scratched, and worn
suitcases for her trip to Birmingham.

Tacky heard a neighbor man enter the house. He and Papa
discussed Tacky's schooling.

"I'm glad that I put Tacky through school," Papa declared.
"Now she can get this college training and find work that'll be
easier for her."

Mama walked in unnoticed. She usually didn't speak up when
Papa spoke with a neighbor, but that day, she said, "Huh! You
didn't put her through school. She put herself through."

Tacky was shocked, but she smiled. She felt sorry for Papa
but was thankful that he was proud of her.

Early Monday morning, Tacky put on her graduation suit,
hightop shoes, and brace. Papa drove her and her suitcases to
Collinsville to catch a bus for Birmingham.

Tacky felt shy and nervous. She'd never been in a big city
before except for the hospital. There were many firsts ahead of
her that day, and she wondered about them.

Tacky

When she stepped down from the bus at the Birmingham depot, she slung her purse across her shoulder. Her booksack hung from her other shoulder, leaving her hands free for the crutches and suitcases. The bus driver looked at her strangely as he set her two suitcases on the platform in front of her. He acted as if he wanted to say something, then thought better of it and walked away.

With a suitcase in each hand and her crutches, Tacky walked to a Traveler's Aid Desk. She knew she looked bundled down, but she hoped she wouldn't have to carry the suitcases too far. "Excuse me, Ma'am. I'm here to attend business college and need to find a room. Can you tell me how to find a place?"

Two kind-looking, gray-haired ladies sat at the desk. They looked at each other in wonder, then one smiled and said, "We'll see what we can do."

"Thank you."

The lady began making calls. After three calls, she said, "Honey, there's a Mrs. Keenman in West Birmingham who keeps girls in her home. She has a vacant room at a low price."

"How would I get there?"

"It happens that I have to go home for lunch and will drive right past there. I can drop you off if you don't mind waiting for thirty minutes," the buxom lady said.

What luck! Tacky thought. "Thank you. I certainly appreciate it. I'll sit out of your way until you're ready."

Tacky chatted with the woman as they drove to look at the room. Tacky, glad it was in a nice neighborhood, offered to pay for the trip, but the lady replied it was on her way home and refused to accept any money.

After unpacking in her room, Tacky spoke with Mrs. Keenman. "I have a prescription for some new hightop shoes I must buy at the Guarantee Shoe Store, then I need to go to the brace shop to have my brace changed. Can you please tell me what streetcars I need to do that?"

"That's no trouble. You can walk down the street a block and a half, then catch 7-A going east. Get off at The Darling Shop, walk down the street to the left you'll see the Guarantee Shoe Store.

"After getting your shoes, continue down the street to the next corner, take a right, and walk two blocks to catch the northbound streetcar. Get off at Twenty-Second Street. The brace shop is on the corner."

.   Tacky had never rode a streetcar before. The directions sounded like Greek to her, but she knew it had to be done. She wrote down the instructions, took a deep breath, picked up her purse, and prepared to go.

Mrs. Keenman handed her a piece of paper. "This is my phone number. If you have any problems, call me, and I'll tell you what to do next."

"Thank you, Ma'am." Tacky left and was surprised how well her trip went. She bought the shoes, found the brace shop, had her brace altered, put the new shoes and brace on, and was ready to retrace her steps home. She felt relieved.

Back at the Darling Shop, she waited across the street for a streetcar going in the opposite direction, but it seemed all 7 A's went east, not west. After half an hour, she mustered her courage and approached a policeman on the corner.

"Pardon me, Sir, can you please tell me where to catch a 7-A going west?"

"Right here at the Darling Shop."

"But that's where I got off coming into town. I want to go the other way."

"Honey, the 7-A makes a loop around several blocks and then turns west."

She thanked him, then felt nervous when she saw the sun sinking in the west. She had a long way to go to return to her room.

Boarding the streetcar, she asked the conductor, "Would you please tell me when we reach Eleventh Avenue west? I've been there only once and it's getting late. I don't know if I'll recognize it again."

"If you'll sit near the front, I'll be glad to tell you." There were no available seats up front, but, as passengers got off, Tacky moved closer until she finally sat near the door.

"This is where you want to get off," the conductor said finally.

"Thank you." Tacky got down and looked around, but nothing seemed familiar. She walked up the street one block, then to the left a block, but she still didn't recognize anything. *Maybe he dropped me off a block too soon,* she thought.

Tacky went up one street and down another, trying to find something that looked familiar, but nothing did. Darkness grew each minute, and she didn't like the looks of the neighborhood.

She saw something up the street that resembled a cafe and remembered Mrs. Keenman's phone number. When she reached the place, she debated if it was safe to enter, but she'd never been so desperate before, so she took a deep breath and walked up to the counter.

"Do you have a phone I can use?" Tacky asked.

"Supply Room." The waitress pointed at a door.

Tacky opened it and went in. She looked around, and saw rats and mice scooting behind the curtains. She wanted to run, but she needed to make her call.

Placing her crutches against the wall near the phone, she took the number from her purse and a dime to pay for the call.

Tacky

She'd never used a phone before and found her hand shaking like a
leaf in a windstorm.

Reading the instructions on the wall, she dropped her dime in
and began dialing the number, watching rats and mice climb
curtains and run around. During the middle of dialing, a big
gopher rat ran between her legs.

Tacky threw down the receiver, slapped her hand over her
mouth to stifle a scream, grabbed her crutches and ran. Once
outside, she fought back tears. It was dark, and she was in a
scary part of the city.

She walked on, asking God to help her find a way back to her
room. A neatly dressed man was on the street a block ahead, so she
followed him. Every time he turned a corner, she hurried as fast
as she could to see where he went.

After many blocks, the neighborhood changed for the better.
At a house down the street, an outside light was on, and a man was
washing his car.

Tacky hurried up to him. "Pardon me, Sir, I'm lost. Do you
have a phone I can use?"

"Yes, there's one inside. Go on in, my wife's in there."

Tacky hesitated, remembering her previous experience. The man
turned off the water. "Come on in. I'll show you where the phone
is."

As he stepped through the door, he called, "Honey? This young
lady says she's lost and wants to use our phone."

"I am sorry to bother you, I'm Lula Mayberry, but everyone
calls me Tacky," she explained. "I'm in Birmingham to attend
business college. I told the streetcar conductor to let me off at
Eleventh Street West. When he did, I was immediately lost."

"He put you off at Eleventh Street North," the woman said.
"How'd you get over here?"

Tacky

"I saw a nicely dressed man and followed him until I saw your
husband washing his car outside."

"I'm putting supper on the table. Will you eat with us?"

"No, thank you.I'm so shaken up, I don't believe I could
swallow a bite."

"Our name's Stammler, and I'm glad you found us. Jacob,
why don't you call for her and find out where she's staying?"
Mrs. Stammler began setting the table.

"Good idea, Sarah."

Tacky handed him the number. He called, got directions, and
said, "If you don't mind waiting until we eat, we'll drive you
back there."

"Go ahead. Eat while it's warm," Tacky replied. I certainly
don't mind waiting."

He smiled and sat down to a table laden with delicious-
smelling food. Tacky saw his eyebrows were as thick and tangled as
marsh grass, but, behind those gold-rimmed glasses, his eyes were
as bright as a terrier's. He had laugh lines at the corners of his
eyes, too.

His wife was a pleasantly plump lady with delicate lips. Her
brown hair had some silver in it, and her eyes were soft and warm.
Tacky thanked God for leading her to a friendly home.

After the meal, the couple drove Tacky to Mrs. Keenman's. On
the way, Tacky worried about the cost, hoping she had enough to
repay them for their kindness.

As they reached the house, she asked, "This is the right
place. What do I owe you kind people for helping me?"

"You go in and bring Mrs. Keenman out so I know we're leaving
you in the right place," Jacob said.

Tacky rang the doorbell, and Mrs. Keenman came out.
Tacky introduced her to her rescuers, assuring them she was in the
right place.

Tacky

"You'll never know how I appreciate your kindness," Tacky
said. "What do I owe you for all the trouble you've gone through
for me?"

"Do you have a Million Dollars?" Mr. Stammler grinned at
her.

"Well, not quite that much."

"Then you don't owe us anything. We're glad you came to our
house, and gave us the opportunity to help."

Tacky went to the car window, put her arms through, and
hugged the man. With tears in her eyes, she said, "I'll always
remember you two as good Samaritans."

He patted her cheek. "We'll remember you, too, Tacky. It's
been our pleasure to help you."

*A country girl's first day in the big city sure has taught me
to watch where I'm going,* Tacky thought, *"Thank You, Lord, for your
loving care through such wonderful, compassionate people. Please
bless each one who had a part in helping me today. In Jesus'
Sweet Name, I pray."*

CHAPTER THIRTEEN

The following morning, Tacky was anxious to begin her college training. Mrs. Keenman told her which streetcar to take and where to get off. She chose landmarks at the places where she got off and on, not wanting a repeat of the previous day.

Tacky was very observant of her location after that terrifying experience. She didn't like being dependent on others to find her way.

She worked hard at typing, shorthand, and bookkeeping, which were new to her. The other subjects were a continuation of classes she studied in high school.

After working hard for eight-and-a-half months, she finished the twelve-month secretarial course with a typing speed of eighty-five words a minute and shorthand speed of 120 words per minute. While waiting for an opening at the Salvation Army, she worked for the administration of the Crippled Children's Clinic.

Mr. Cavalier and the major at the Salvation Army were good friends. When the major needed a secretary, Tacky got the job—another way God was looking out for her.

Tacky, a little country girl from a small country church, felt like an ant sitting in a corner in the huge congregations of the Methodist and Baptist Churches she visited.

Major, her boss, worked with the young people who had wiener roasts, swimming parties, and get-togethers at Church and at the different people's homes. He invited Tacky to join in those outings. Before becoming involved in their fellowship, she decided to attend services first. She didn't know much about the Salvation Army, except that General Booth, the founder, was a Methodist who started a new organization when his church didn't like his bringing in outcasts and alcoholics to the services.

Instead, General Booth began the work he felt the Lord called him to do. Soup, *Soap, and Salvation,* became his motto. Tacky learned the Salvation Army's doctrine was sound and enjoyed their services. Major was a good preacher--kind, compassionate, and loving with people of all ages. At the swimming parties, he bowed his legs and croaked like a frog as he dove into the water, entertaining little children who screamed, "Do it again, Major!" He did until he was exhausted.

Sometimes, he put a youngster on his back, swam around, and said, "Under we go!" The kids learned to hold their breath that way. He had an incredible gift of friendship that made all children, young people, and adults love to be with him. Tacky felt honored that God placed her within such a lovely family.

She enjoyed her office work, and life was full of a sense of joy and happiness unlike anything she knew before. She slowly lost some of her timidity. Tillie, the other office worker, was a middle-aged, semi-plump lady with short, light-brown hair streaked with gray, and tender, hazel eyes. They sparkled with a mischievous twinkle, showing many years of kindness and fun.

Tacky

From Tacky's first day in the office, Tillie was like a
helpful mother to her. With love and kindness, she trained Tacky
in her duties, and Tacky soon felt completely at home with such
wonderful people.

Tacky felt like David, the Psalmist, who said, "Praise ye
the Lord. O give thanks unto the Lord, for He is good, for His
mercy endureth forever," (Psalms 106:1).

Tacky couldn't wait to write Cran, Mama, and Papa and tell
them how blessed she was at work. After a few paydays, Tacky
moved to a new boarding room.

She took a room with Dr. and Mrs. Grey who lived a block
and a half from Mrs. Keenman. They had two upstairs rooms they
rented to working girls. Since one was available and was cheaper
than Mrs. Keenman's, Tacky took it.

Dr. Grey was a tall, straight, raw-boned man, in his early
seventies, with gray-streaked hair and a mischievous glint in his
clear, blue eyes that showed his sense of humor. The lines around
the corners of his mouth gave Tacky the feeling Dr. Grey received
a lot from life and was eager to return even more to it.

Mrs. Grey was a buxom woman with rosy cheeks and eyes that
were as warm as the summer sun or as cold as a bleak winter ice
storm. She spent most of her time reading or watching T.V.
Although the living room was kept neat, her bedroom was piled high
with newspapers and magazines.

Many evenings when Tacky came in from work, she found Mrs.
Grey reading or watching T.V.

"Tacky, there's plenty of food on the stove if you're
hungry," Mrs. Grey said, knowing Tacky would clean the kitchen if
she ate. Sometimes, Tacky had already eaten, but she cleaned the
kitchen, anyway.

Tacky

One evening when Tacky came home from work, she started
upstairs to her room, but Mrs. Grey said, "Tacky, come here a
minute. I want to discuss something with you."

The other two boarders never spent much time with the Greys.
They told Tacky, "Mrs. Grey will use you, if you let her. That's
why we never talk to her."

Tacky entered the living room to see what she wanted.

"How was your day at work?" Mrs. Grey asked.

"Fine. I love working with Tillie and Major. They're kind,
sweet, and very understanding. You said you had something to
discuss. Have I done something wrong?"

"Oh, heavens, no! It isn't anything like that. I want to
make a trade with you."

"A trade? what kind of trade?"

"Well, you know we have a daughter that lives in New York.
She wants us to come up and spend a couple weeks with her. I
spoke with Dr. Grey, but he doesn't feel he can leave his
patients. However, he said if I could talk you into cooking for
him, it would be all right for me to go."

"If he thinks he can eat my cooking, I'll be glad to cook for
him while you're away." Tacky smiled.

"If you'll cook his breakfast and dinner each morning and
evening, we'll give you your meals and room free, while I'm away."

Tacky thought, *That gives me the chance to double my
payments to Papa, then Cran and I can get married even sooner.* "I
don't know if he'll like my cooking, but I'll do my best."

"He isn't hard to please."

From what Tacky had seen Mrs. Grey cook, she knew that was
true.

The first morning after Mrs. Grey left, Tacky went into the
kitchen to cook breakfast. Mrs. Grey left some brown and serve
rolls with meat and eggs. Tacky never cooked on a gas stove

before. When she buttered the tops of the rolls and put them in to brown, she took up the sausage and put the eggs on to cook.

She turned around and saw smoke coming from the oven. Grabbing a pot holder, she took the burned rolls from the oven and quickly looked for more, but there weren't any.

What in the world will I do? she wondered. She quickly made homemade biscuits and popped them into the oven.

Dr. Grey came downstairs and asked, "Worshipping early, aren't you?"

"I beg your pardon?" she asked in confusion.

"Offering up burned sacrifices." His eyes smiled.

Tacky's face blazed! "Dr. Grey, I'm so sorry I burned your rolls. There weren't any more, so I made biscuits. I hope you don't mind. I've never cooked on a gas stove before. It heats up a lot faster than I anticipated."

Tacky checked her biscuits and found they were ready. She put Dr. Grey's sausage, eggs, and blackberry jelly from their farm on the table, poured a cup of coffee, and handed him the freshly baked biscuits.

He gave thanks for the food they were about to eat, then took a bite of a biscuit. "I've never been so happy with burned rolls in my life, Tacky. These biscuits hit the spot. Will you please cook them every morning for me?"

Greatly relieved, she said, "I'll be glad to."

He smiled at her. "These are the first homemade biscuits I've had in years."

When Tacky came in from work that afternoon, she looked through the refrigerator and pantry to see what she could prepare for dinner. She found some leftover chicken in the fridge, and, since she'd been taught to never let anything go to waste, she decided to make chicken potpie and salad.

She peeled a carrot, an onion, some potatoes, and boiled them until tender, then opened a can of peas, and one of corn, mixing them together. She deboned the chicken, cut it into little pieces, and mixed it with some vegetables. After dissolving a chicken bouillon cube in vegetable broth, she sprinkled in black pepper, a little cornstarch, and Worchester sauce. She made a nice, tender crust for the bottom, browned it until almost done, poured in the filling, and placed a crust over the top before baking it while she cut up lettuce and made a salad. Finally, she made tea and set the table.

Dr. Grey got off work an hour after Tacky, and she had dinner ready when he arrived. As he entered the house he called, "What's the tantalizing aroma coming from the kitchen?"

Tacky laughed. "Smells better than burnt sacrifice this morning, eh?"

As they ate, Dr. Grey said, "When Mrs. Grey calls onight, I'll tell her she can stay another week. I like your cooking."

"Even if I began by burning your rolls?"

"Even then. That was one of the greatest blessings I've had in years," he laughed.

Tacky enjoyed cooking for him. He had a ravenous appetite and was very complimentary.

She couldn't go home often, because she sent most of her money home every payday to repay Papa. She wrote Cran every few days, including glowing reports of her work and new residence. She let him know how thriftly she was saving so they could be together soon. He wrote back and longed for the day when she'd become his wife.

Teresa and Peter occasionally sent her a few dollars to ride the bus to Gadsden to spend the weekend with them. Cran met her there, and they enjoyed a wonderful time together. Tacky caught a late bus back, trying to stay with her family as long as possible. Cran begged her to return home so they could marry, but she was determined to repay her debt to Papa first.

Mama told her when she began sending the money each week that what Papa spent on her wasn't as much as he led most peole to believe. The insurance covered the hospital bill, and Dr. Sommerset charged only what the insurance would pay, plus an occasional pork ham or shoulder.

After Tacky's fifth surgery, the Crippled Children's Clinic took over, so Papa didn't have to pay for any future surgeries. Mostly, he was out his transportation, meal and costs for driving back and forth when you were in the hospital.

Tacky and Cran corresponded regularly. His letters were filled with intense longing for the time when they'd be together. They worked hard and saved all they could for that time.

One of the lady Salvation Army officer's was transferred to another city, which left the house with only one other girl living there. Major told Tacky if she wanted to move in with Barbara, she could eat with her at the emergency home next door, and thus save her room rent and meal expenses.

Tacky immediately wrote Cran that the Lord was making a way for them soon to become one, and she was very excited.

Major and Mrs. Wilkin's daughter, Dean, married in November, 1945. They had a simple, but beautiful ceremony at the Salvation Army church. Major knew that Tacky and Cran wanted to marry soon, too, and he wanted to officiate.

He told her he'd give her the same kind of wedding she'd just seen, if she'd let him marry them. Tacky wanted to talk it over with Cran, who was a very timid soul, so she doubted he'd allow it. She loved Major and his family dearly and appreciated how they included her in many things as one of the family, but she didn't want to make Cran feel bad, either. She loved him and

wanted to become a devoted wife who considered her husband's
feelings before her own. She looked forward to a bright future
with Cran but dreaded telling Papa they were getting married.

CHAPTER FOURTEEN

After moving into the house with Barbara, Tacky would be able to send more money to Papa. When she was able to visit her family again, she announced she planned to marry Cranston very soon.

Papa said, "Tacky, I appreciate the money you've sent, but you've paid more than you should. I don't approve of Cranston. I hoped you'd find a doctor or lawyer, someone who'd give you an easier life, but you seem set on this. If you make your bed hard, you'll have to sleep in it."

Tacky grinned, went to him, and hugged him. "Papa, where would I find a more honest, upright man, let alone a harder worker?"

"I know, but I'm still a little disappointed. One Knox in the family is enough."

"Don't be. I would rather marry a man I love, who loves me, and is honest and upright, than to have all the money in the world." She hugged him again.

Cran and Tacky set their wedding date for January 19,1946, but Cran didn't want a church wedding.

"I don't believe I could ever make it through a service like that," he pleaded.

"That's fine. We want to begin our marriage by agreeing, not disagreeing."

They asked Tacky's nephew and girlfriend, whom they double-dated with for years, if they'd like to make it a double, and they agreed.

Two miles south of Collinsville the bus always stopped for thirty minutes.

"I'll pick you up at the rest stop," Cran told Tacky. "Then you won't have to wait."

"That would be nice."

Saturday, January 19th, finally arrived. Tacky wanted to look her best, so she went to the beauty shop to get her hair done. She always did it herself but thought it would look better if done by a professional. When she came home and looked in the mirror, she could have cried.

She combed it out and started all over, finally finding a style that was more like her. She was thankful she had time to finish before catching the bus.

She usually took a streetcar to the bus station, but she packed her suitcase for more than a weekend, so, for this special occasion, she called a cab. Soon, the long-awaited ceremony would take place, and she and Cran would begin their lives together. She was so excited!

When she reached the rest stop, Cran wasn't there. Tacky waited a long time. When the bus came for Collinsville, Tacky boarded it again.

Once at the bus station, Cran wasn't there, either, so Tacky felt anxious. Cran was never late, and it was their wedding day. She couldn't imagine what happened.

After walking to the door many times, she finally saw Cran's old truck rattling around the corner. He jumped out and ran inside, covered in grease. He didn't dare hug her like that.

"What in the world happened? I had just about decided I had been jilted!" Tacky teased.

"You know better than that. Halfway between here and the rest stop, I had a flat tire, and rushed like mad to fix it and get there in time, but I didn't make it. Didn't you see me on the side of the road as the bus passed?"

"No, I was too disappointed to look," she admitted.

"I'm sorry, Honey. You should've known something happened, or I would've been there."

They went to the hotel where he and Dub rented rooms and explained the situation to the manager. He gave them a key to both rooms, and Tacky showered and dressed in one while Cran cleaned up and dressed in the other. Then they met Dub and Tress at the designated place, and all drove to Rising Fawn, Georgia, to a double wedding conducted by a justice of the peace.

After the ceremony, the justice of the peace said, "You brides must always meet your husband at the door with a smile, a hug, and a tender kiss. Butterflies will swarm around your door, and birds will sing happily around your windows, echoing your happiness."

Tress and Tacky exchanged a look and giggled.

Cran was a tender, loving husband. He enjoyed being loved, and touched. He liked lying on the couch with his head in Tacky's lap, while she combed his hair or patted his face.

Tacky had enough of Papa in her that it was hard for her to be as demonstrative with her affection as she wanted—or Cran desired. With his tenderness, and persuasion, she learned the art of expressing her love through little touches and acts of attention. When they were riding in the car, he wanted her hand on his arm or knee. He almost glowed when she patted or squeezed him.

While on their honeymoon, Cran received a call to come in for his examination for the Armed Services even though he'd been exempted for farming. When he left for the examination, Tacky returned to work.

Cran didn't return home after that. He was shipped directly to Neosha, Missouri, to begin his six-week bivouac training. That was a great disappointment for both of them!

He wrote her every day telling her about his training, how hard and strenuous it was, and how he loved and missed her. Tacky's heart ached for him. She wanted to be there to rub his aching muscles and comfort him. He wouldn't get a weekend off until he finished the six weeks' training. Both of them counted the days.

Finally, after what felt like six months but was only six weeks, Cran called one Wednesday night to ask Tacky to meet him in Neosha for the weekend.

She asked Major if she could get off from work Friday to be ready when Cran finished his work.

"If I can carry your luggage for you," Major teased. "I wouldn't miss this for anything."

She wired for hotel reservations, but the first two wired back with the words, *Sorry. No Vacancy.* Maybe the other young men reserved the rooms first.

Then the third request came back with the words, *Reservation Confirmed,* and she was ecstatic. She could hardly wait for Friday.

Thursday morning as Tacky and Barbara walked to work, Tacky hopped and skipped as best one could with a brace on her leg, singing and acting out her pent-up energy and joy, "I'm going to see my husband!"

"It's good to see you so happy," Barbara said. "I know how lonely you've been without Cran."

They laughed with great anticipation and excitement.

As they rounded a corner one block from the office, they saw a telegram boy knocking on the office door.

"I hope they haven't canceled our reservation," Tacky said.

"No, they just cancelled Cran's week-end pass." Barbara teased.

"Oh! Don't say such a thing!"

The delivery boy, seeing them coming, came to meet them. "I have a priority telegram for Mrs. Lula Knox."

Tacky looked at the telegram, which had the word *Priority* on it in big letters. "Why would it be priority?"

"Why don't you open it and see?" Barbara asked.

Tacky laughed, and stuck out her tongue at her friend, and signed for the telegram. Nothing could dampen her spirits on such a special day.

She ripped it open and read the message.

"Your husband, Cranston E. Knox, seriously ill, Stop. Spinal menigitis. Stop. Come at once. Stop. Recovery questionable. Stop.

Signed: Captain Trulock

"This isn't possible," Tacky said in shock. "I spoke with him last night. He said he had an ear infection, but it wasn't anything serious."

Tacky unlocked the Office, went into the ladies' lounge, lay down on the couch and burst into tears.

Major came in, and Barbara showed him the telegram. He immediately called Captain Trulock and confirmed that Cran was in critical condition and didn't look like he'd survive.

Major wanted someone to go with Tacky but she knew she'd control herself better if she were alone. She would worry about asking someone for a favor too.

Tacky

He checked with the airport and found all planes between
Birmingham and Neosha were grounded due to stormy weather,
so he and Tillie closed the office. He went to the the train depot
and bought a train ticket for Tacky, then he and Tillie took Tacky
home to pack.

As he gave her the ticket, he asked, "Won't you please change
your mind and let someone come with you?"

"Thank you, Major, for your concern. I appreciate it, but
it's best I go alone. I'll call when I arrive and tell you what I
find out."

"Make sure you do. If you need money or any other kind of
help, I hope you feel free to call on me as if I were your father.
You can reach us anytime. I know how difficult it is for you to
reach your folks, so please let us know if we can help."

"Major, you're so very sweet. I promise to let you know if I
need help."

Suddenly, Tacky realized that if she needed help, she felt
freer to ask Major than Papa, mostly because he had more money
available for emergencies. That was a great comfort to know Major
was there if she needed someone.

*One doesn't realize the true value of a friend until they need
help,* Tacky thought.

When she arrived at the train depot in Neosha, an Army
lieutenant was waiting to pick her up and take her to the
Army hospital where a nurse directed her to Cran's room.

Just outside the door was a rack of caps, gowns, gloves, and
masks that people donned before entering the room. When they
emerged later, they had to wash in disinfectant.

When Tacky finally saw Cran, she was shocked. The doctor was
changing an ice pack over his eyes, which were swollen almost out
of their sockets, and his neck rigid and straight. Both head and
neck looked ready to burst. The nurse tried to warn Tacky before

Tacky

she entered the room, but she still wasn't prepared for such a drastic sight.

Two doctors had been working on Cran for twenty-four hours straight, keeping ice compresses on his eyes to prevent them from bursting.

Captain Trulock introduced himself and warned Tacky to expect anything. He added she shouldn't come too close until they saw how Cran reacted to her presence. She spoke his name without getting a response, then asked if she could touch him.

"Yes, but be very careful," a doctor said. "Be prepared to get out of the way if he reacts violently."

Tacky couldn't imagine Cran reacting violently to her.

"Sometimes," the doctor added,"that's what happens when the person they love most sees them in this state."

Tacky walked closer and placed a cool hand on Cran's forehead. "Cran, Honey, it's Tacky. I've come to help you get better."

He stirred and moaned. Tacky talked to him for a while.

"You'd better go to your room and get some rest," Captain Trulock said. I know this has been an extremely hard trip for you. I've arranged for you here in the hospital. You can take your meals in the hospital mess hall with the doctors and nurses. Lieutenant Jeffery will show you to your room. Dinner's at five o'clock. She'll also show you how to find the mess hall. You can visit your husband again after dinner. Get some rest."

Tacky thanked him and followed Lieutenant Jeffery to her room, silently thanking God for such warm, kind people. Finding a pay phone near her room, Tacky called Major to let him know she arrived safely. Major gave her many warm messages from friends, and from people she hardly knew, saying they were praying for Cran. Tacky appreciated that. It was clear that it would take God's help to save Cran's life.

Tacky

Each day she sat beside Cran as long as the doctors allowed, which was longer than for most patients in his condition. As she held his hand and rubbed his fevered brow, Cran's restless tossing and turning became calm.

Tacky prayed while she rubbed his hand or forehead. Her faith And hope never waivered, even when the doctors said there was very little hope left.

"I know,"Tacky replied, "but God can do what doctors can't."

"That's true," Captain Trulock said. Hold onto your faith."

Cran's six-foot-two-inch, 180-pound frame looked very delicate, replacing the stout, strong body Tacky rememberd. Having been raised on a farm, working in the open all his life, and eating plenty of fresh vegetables made him a healthy young man.

"That's the only thing that's kept him alive so long," the doctors said. "The average person wouldn't have survived. However, we want you to realize he's not out of the woods yet."

The hours she spent sitting with Cran were long and lonely, but Tacky knew to trust God for the necessary strength. He would supply peace even in the midst of a storm, which was how she felt.

Two weeks later Cran regained consciousness and began improving rapidly.

"Mrs. Knox," Captain Trulock said, "we're supposed to send you home as soon as he regained consciousness, but since you live so far away, and all his letters would have to be sterilized before we could mail them, I'll let you stay the rest of the week. I don't want you going home just to worry."

Tacky shook his hand and smiled. "Captain, you have been more than generous to me. I'll always remember your kindness. Thank you so much."

"Well, I'm from Georgia," he said, laughing. "That makes us almost neighbors."

Tacky

Tacky returned to work the first day of the following week. It was several days before letters arrived from Cran, and he improved so fast, the doctors were amazed. They'd never seen anything like it. At first, they told Tacky that even if Cran survived, he'd never be able to lift more than a ten-pound sack of potatoes, and he'd never be able to hold down a strenuous job.

Three months after Tacky returned, she received another letter from Cran. In it, he wrote, *They're giving me a two-week pass to come home before shipping me overseas.*

"I can't believe they're shipping Cran overseas for active duty so soon," Tacky told Major. "Why, they told me a few months ago, he'd never do hard work again."

"Don't underestimate the Power of the Lord."

"I know. I remember all those prayers that were going up for him. Almost every person I met when I came home would say, *Tacky, we're been praying for you and your husband.* That really means a lot to me."

Major looked at Tacky's thin, childlike body, and said, "When he arrives, I want you to leave with him. We don't want to see you back here until he goes back to camp."

"Really! You mean I can have some time off?"

"I mean we don't want to see you around until he leaves." Major smiled.

"Oh, Major, you're too good to me! You're so understanding. You'll never know how much I appreciate all of you. God was good to give me such wonderful people to work with."

"Stop crying, Tacky. You'll have to work twice as hard to make it up when you return."

The two weeks with Cran passed so quickly, Tacky almost didn't realize it. Soon, it was time for him to catch a train for California, where he'd rejoin his company to be shipped overseas.

"Tacky, just tell me goodbye here at your apartment,"

he said, holding her tenderly.

"Oh Cran, I can't bear not going as far with you as I can," Tacky whispered, as tears welled up in her clear blue eyes.

"I know, Honey, and I want you with me all the way, but It'll be hard for you to watch me get on the train."

"It will, but I want to be with you every minute I can." She gave him her winning smile.

Cran put his strong arms around her, holding her tightly. "How I wish I didn't have to leave you. Maybe it won't be too long until we can be together and begin our lives as Mr. and Mrs. Knox. Won't that be wonderful?"

"Terrific. I'll be counting the days." She stretched up on tipitoe to kiss him.

"Promise you'll take care of yourself. You're so thin, I want to be here to take care of you instead of being so far away."

"Oh, I'm fine. Don't you worry a minute about me. You're the one who'll be in danger. We'll have to trust God to take care of both of us and bring us together soon." She smiled up at him, her blue eyes glistening with tears.

"That's true, darling." He held her tightly as the cab arrived to take them to the train station.

At the station, when people began boarding the train, Cran said, "Tacky, please don't cry. I can't stand to leave you if you cry."

"Oh, I won't. I'll just wave and wave until you're out of sight." Tacky smiled. She kissed him goodbye, as the train whistle blew for the last call, and he hopped aboard. He got a seat near the window and waved until the train pulled out of sight.

As it rounded a curve where Tacky could no longer see Cran, she could hold the tears back no longer. A large part of herself was leaving on that train, and she felt empty inside.

Tacky

When would she see him again? What would the future hold for
them?

Oh, Lord, please take care of him, she prayed. She wrote Cran
every night and worked hard during the days. Office work had
piled up while she was away for two weeks, and she was glad
to have something to keep her occupied.

After she caught up with her work, she looked for something
else to do to keep busy. She didn't want to have time to think
about her loneliness.

After Thanksgiving, she donned a Salvation Army uniform
at night and went with the other church youth selling War
Cry's, (a Special Christmas Edition of their Christian Magazine),
to raise money to help the needy at Christmas.

They went out in pairs from house to house selling the
magazine. Some people were very nice and gave a few dollars,
because they wanted to help in the Salvation Army's benevolent
work. Occasionally, someone would curse them out and slam the
door in their face. About the time one would become very
discouraged and feel like quitting, someone would be very nice and
give a large donation, saying "I have been looking forward to your
visit so I could help in this worthy cause."

Tacky enjoyed going out with the group, which helped fill
more lonely time with worthwhile work.

A week before Christmas Tacky received a telegram from Cran.
"Just landed in U.S...Will be home for Christmas." Signed, "Your
loving, anxious husband, Cran."

Major was on a downtown street corner, playing Christmas
carols as he rang the bell at the tripod that held a pot for
donations.

Tacky read the telegram and told Tillie, "I can't wait to
share the good news with Major."

"Yes, by all means go and spread the good news!"

111

Tacky

Tacky hurried as fast as her braced leg allowed.

When she saw Major, she waved the telegram in the air, and he hurried toward her.

"Is something wrong?" he asked.

"No! Everything is right!" She handed it to him.

Major read it, put his arm around Tacky, and danced a little Jig. He walked over to change the record to I'll Be Home For Christmas, by Bing Crosby.

Tears of joy trickled down Tacky's cheeks. She could hardly wait to see Cran.

"I'm very happy for you," Major said. I don't know why, though. When Cran returns, you'll leave the office again, and it'll be a sad time for all of us, but we want you to be happy, too," he said, as he patted her shoulder.

Tacky listened day and night for the phone call that would tell her Cran would be home. She worked long hard hours at the office to get the year-end work up-to-date, so she wouldn't leave anything dragging when Cran came home.

Christmas Eve came and no phone call. Her hopes of Cran making it home for Christmas dwindled fast.

Just as she was walking out the door to go to the Office for the last few details, the buzzer went off, signaling that she had a phone call next door. Buzzz...Buzzzzzzz....Buzzzzzzzzz! She knew it was Cran, for they never put so much emphasis on her phone calls before!

She took off running...It was Cran! " Where are you?" she asked, delighted to hear his voice.

"At the train depot...I am taking a cab out, and just wanted to know if you were home or at work!"

"Home; hurry, I can hardly wait... I was beginning to lose all hopes that you would be here for Christmas!" She said excitedly.

"Me, too." Cran agreed.

Tacky relayed the good news to the Emergency Home Employees
and rushed over to the apartment, Sunday Papers were strewn over
the living room. She wanted it to be tidy, so she began picking
up papers, running to the window to see if the cab had arrived.

She picked papers from the couch, ran to the window, laid
them on a table, went back to the window, picked them up again
laid them in a chair. She was so excited, she hardly knew what she
was doing. When the cab arrived, she flew out the door into the
strong arms of her six-foot-two-inch, 200 pound, muscular husband.

Cran picked her up as though she were an infant, swung her
around, hugging, kissing, and squeezing her. The Cab Driver just
cut the motor off and sat there grinning. When she realized this,
Tacky's face turned red; she waved to the driver, and led her
long-awaited husband into the house.

"We have lots of catching up to do." Cran said as he hugged
her tight and picked her up to carry her over the threshold.
Tacky laughed.

"Put me down. That cab driver is still sitting there looking
at us," she said.

"Who cares? If it had been almost a year since he saw his
wife, he'd be excited, too." Cran smiled as he pulled her to his
big strong body, planting a kiss on her forehead and then to her
lips, and squeezing her tightly to him.

"Tacky, you don't know how many times I have dreamed of this
moment. Just to hold you tightly and never let you go. That's
what kept me going. I love you so much."

"I know, Cran, I dreamed, too. Now we can begin our life
together. I can hardly wait until we have our own home. Won't
that be wonderful?"

"I say it will, Darling!! We'll start building it right
away! Now I'd like to Wish you a Merry Christmas, Mrs. Knox."

Tacky

"Oh, I had almost forgotten that tomorrow is Christmas. Merry Christmas to you, too. Isn't it wonderful to be together for our first Christmas?"

"I'll say."

Tacky

CHAPTER FIFTEEN

Tacky and Cran visited their families during the Christmas
holidays, and hunted a house to rent until they could build. They
found a small, three-room shack across the creek from Papa and
Mama. The kitchen floor had cracks so wide, the cold winter air
came right through. Tacky had to wear heavy socks, high-top shoes
and an overshoe over her brace to keep from freezing while she
cooked.

As soon as she finished breakfast, she went into the living
room, which also served as their bedroom, where there was a big
coal heater. She pulled off her shoes to rub some feeling into her
cold toes and feet. She would smile as she thought of the steam
heated house she left in Birmingham, where she didn't even
have to sleep under a quilt.

What a person won't do for love, she thought.

Cran bought an acre of washed-away land from the corner
of Peter & Teresa's land. He bought a dump truck and hauled
rock and dirt and filled in a huge ditch that just about cut
the acre in half until it was level ground again, not a washed-
away hill. Then he bought a barrack building at Camp

Siebert, in Gadsden, where the Army was selling all the unused barracks.

Cran tore it down, hauled the lumber, windows, and doors to his new land, and Tacky pulled nails from the lumber before stacking the pieces by size. She drew plans for the five-room house with closets in each room she wanted, and they built the first room.

Peter couldn't imagine why anyone would want so many closets. His house had only one.

"I like lots of storage room." Tacky told Cran.

"Well, now is the time to decide what you want," he said.

Tacky had trouble with her reproductive system. The doctors said those organs hadn't developed due to her fight with osteomyelitis during puberty.

"Pregnancy is the only thing that will correct your current problems," her doctor explained.

After minor surgery, the doctor gave her medication to help her conceive. She and Cran were so excited when she finally became pregnant. She felt sick and threw up constantly, though, unable to keep anything down, including liquids. She had to be fed intravenously and needed injections to keep from losing the baby.

Even though she was ill and weak most of the time, if she could sit up, she sat on a pile of lumber and pulled nails to help Cran get the lumber ready for building.

They framed and put up outside walls and a roof, then put in ceiling on three rooms before they moved in on July fourth. It was a thrill to finally be in their own home, even though they had to keep building the rest of it.

Tacky threatened to miscarry and needed more injections. She was constantly nauseous and vomited often during the entire nine months.

The house was finished just before Christmas, and Etheridge was born on New Year's Day 1948. When that little bundle of life was placed in her arms, Tacky thought, *What a miracle! Oh, God, please give us the wisdom to guide this little life You placed in our care. Help us show him love and instill love for You in his heart, so you can use him in Your Kingdom work*

"Cran, he's so beautiful and precious," Tacky whispered. "He looks just like you."

"Precious, yes, but I'm not sure about beautiful. He's so wrinkled, he looks like he has enough skin for two babies."

"That's because I couldn't keep my food down. He'll fill out soon, and even you will agree he's the most beautiful baby in the county."

When the nurse came in, Cran asked her, "Are you sure he's all right? He's so tall and wrinkled."

The nurse laughed. "Just give him a few weeks. He'll fill in and will be a very roly poly little fellow. He hasn't had the easiest situation in which to develop the past nine months, but he's still a perfect specimen even if he's wrinkled. Look at his frame."

When they took Etheridge home from the hospital, the nurse dressed him in the little outfit Tacky made and handed him to Cran to carry, who held both arms straight out. She laughed. "You don't carry a baby like a load of wood. Cradle your arm and let his head lie against your chest. He won't break."

Cran was thrilled to have a son, but he feared to pick him up, thinking he was fragile.

Bathing him was a delightful time for Tacky. She placed a towel across her lap, and bathed his little face, eyes, nose and ears, then on down his body, so tenderly. She rubbed him down with baby lotion and powder, turned him on his stomach, massaging his back, spanking him gently from head to toe, Cran feared she might hurt him, and Papa said the boy would never know when he got a spanking later in life, because she spanked him so much loving him as a baby.

Etheridge grew and filled out so quickly. Soon, his wrinkles were gone, and Tacky wondered how life could hold such joy and wonder. Each knew day was special.

Cran got a job driving a delivery truck for American Bakeries, and their lives were filled with hard work and plenty of joy. Tacky always had a good meal waiting for Cran when he returned home from work. She thanked God that the Spinal Meningitis hadn't left him crippled as the doctors said. He seemed to be as strong as ever. The only difference in Cran was that his right eyelid drooped over his eye, because he couldn't close the lid completely.

CHAPTER SIXTEEN

Years passed quickly. One Christmas, Cran went to the woods to cut a large cedar, fixed a stand, and the family decorated the tree with items Tacky made. Cran bought Etheridge a little red tricycle and a big yellow truck he could sit on and pedal around with his feet. They couldn't wait until Christmas morning, when he saw his presents.

"Oh, Eppy! Come see what Santa brought you!" Cran lifted him from his baby bed, and set him down in the doorway so he could see the Christmas tree and new toys.

Sensing his parents' excitement, he squealed, "OOOOOH, WEEE!" He looked at the toys, then ran to a Prince Albert tobacco can his Granddaddy had given him to play with many weeks earlier. He hugged it to his chest, and said, "Toy!"

Cran and Tacky looked at each other and the toys they sacrificed to buy, then realized that love and excitement made a home, not toys.

When Eppy was two, they began planning for another child. Michael was born December 16, 1950, just before Eppy turned three.

Tacky's doctor brought his nurse to the house to deliver the baby at home. A friend of Tacky's had just had her baby at home, and Tacky thought that would allow her to stay with Eppy, but she had many complications, and blood poisoning set in.

Cran had to get another doctor to take over and perform surgery on Tacky. In the end, she had to leave both sons for a while.

Tacky found a lump in her breast when Mike was born, and she had the doctor who delivered the baby examine it. He said it was a stopped-up milk gland and wasn't worried.

Still, the breast gave her much trouble, and it became swollen with red streaks in it. She wasn't one to go to the doctor unless she was ill, so she put up with it until Mike was eight months old. Finally, the breast hurt so much, she had to see someone.

Dr. Gross wanted to put Tacky in surgery immediately. He found a large mass in her breast, though he wasn't sure if it was cancer.

He wanted Dr. Moore, an oncologist, to perform the operation. Dr. Moore found a tumor with a four-inch span of roots intermingled with the milk glands.

"If this doesn't come back within five years, you're safe," he told Cran and Tacky.

Cran's hobby was reworking old, washed-out yards into beautiful settings. He bought dump trucks and landscaping equipment and soon had an extra job.

In November before Michael was born, Cran planted a doctor's yard. The doctor traded him an old upright piano for part of his payment.

When Cran brought it home, Tacky thought, "What in the world do we need with a piano? None of us knows how to play.

Tacky

A niece was visiting a few days later and picked out a jingle with one finger, "I can read, I can write, I can smoke my daddy's pipe!"

When Eppy heard it, he went to the piano and played it with both hands, then began playing Jesus Loves Me, and all the little songs he heard sung over the radio to a children's program. Tacky and Cran stood back with mouths opened in amazement.

Cran grabbed Tacky hugging her and said, "Now, do you wonder why I traded for the piano?"

The piano grew to be one of their favorite instruments. Anything Eppy heard, he could play. Many evenings, after a hard day's work, they gathered around the piano and sang as Eppy played.

One evening Tacky said, "What shall we sing tonight?"

Eppy said, "Sing Leaning on the Elastic Arms."

Cran laughed while Tacky hugged the boy. "That's a good name for that song. After all, God's arms are elastic as well as everlasting, reaching down from heaven to earth to encircle people around the world."

Michael grew into a plump fellow, full of fun and laughter, running over with mischief.

Eppy was more serious. The house became a mixture of seriousness, mischief, fun, and laughter, along with the continuing series of surgeries Tacky endured.

One day when Eppy was four, they were backing the car from the driveway to go into town when he patted her shoulder and said, "Stop, Mom! I gotta go, I gotta go!" Tacky stopped, and Eppy ran into the house. Tacky thought he had to use the bathroom, but she soon heard him playing, Lily of the Valley. When a tune came into that boy's head, he became obsessed by it and couldn't wait to see if he could play it. Often, as he played in the sand with his toy cars and trucks, he would jump up and take off as fast as his little legs would carry him, to the piano to play some particular song he had heard. By the time he was five, he played and sang each Thursday morning for their Pastor's radio program.

Michael loved crawling under the trucks and tractors to help Cran fix them. The greasier he got, the better he liked it. He thoroughly enjoyed being with Daddy wherever he went. The work was never too hard or too dirty to suit him, even as a chubby little tyke. HE was always getting hurt because he was so active, always trying something he wasn't old enough to do.

One day, Eppy chopped tree branches to make a small fire for roasting marshmallows. He kept missing the limb with the hatchet, so Mike moved the branch over just as he came down with the hatchet. It struck a glancing blow and sliced the meat off the end of one of Mike's fingers. Tacky fearing tendon damage, took him to the emergency room.

Cran was proud of his boys, but he wanted a little girl, too. Wherever they went, if there was a little girl he asked Tacky, "Isn't she cute? Wouldn't you give anything if she were ours? How about us adopting a little girl to go with our boys? This would make our home complete."

Tacky had so much trouble delivering her two sons, and her health was so frail, they didn't plan to have any more children. She needed several operations to remove tumors from her breast and reproductive organs.

On Thanksgiving before Mike was two, the family went to Mama's sister's for a big Thanksgiving feast. On the way home, Tacky was so sick, Cran had to stop several times to let her throw up.

"If I didn't know better, I'd declare I was pregnant," Tacky said, getting back into the car and lying her head on the seat.

Tacky

"You just overate. You'll be OK tomorrow. You can't get
pregnant, but wouldn't it be wonderful if you were, and the Lord
sent us a little girl?"

She was too ill to answer. In December, Cran returned home
from work one night and carried Tacky to the hospital's emergency
room. The staff gave her shots and suppositories to stop her
nausea.

She felt better at two o'clock that morning, so they let her
return home. Halfway home, though, she became sick again, and Cran
had to pull over. Tacky felt embarrassed.

"Cran, just drive slowly," she said. "Let me hang my head out
the window. People will think we're drunks upchucking."

It turned out she was pregnant. She was in the hospital
every few weeks. At times, she vomited until blood came. It looked
as if Cran might lose her despite everything the doctors did. He
stayed with her until midnight one night. When she was resting a
little better, he returned home to check on Mama and the boys.

Brother Waits, their pastor, awoke about one o'clock feeling
very concerned about Tacky, got up, dressed, and went to the
hospital.

Tacky became so sick after Cran left that she began retching
again.

She vomited fresh blood all over the bed, and reached for a
glass of water to rinse her mouth, but she was so weak, she
knocked the pitcher over, spilling water on the bed.

When Brother Waits walked in and saw her as white as the
sheets and looking completely limp with blood and water
everywhere, he thought she was dead. Taking her hand, he detected
a faint pulse and rang for the nurse, then he started praying for
her.

Tacky

He was looking for a phone so he could call Cran when he met him walking down the hall.

Cran, who'd been worried, decided to return to visit Tacky again that night.

"Cran, you need to get Tacky to a doctor. She is going to die. Her doctor doesn't seem to be doing a thing," her Pastor said.

About that time Dr. Gross walked in, looking weary and worn.

He took Cran's hand and said, "Mr. Knox your wife is in very critical condition, as I'm sure you already realize. I have been calling all night, everywhere I could think of or anywhere anyone referred me, to try to find someone who could give me some suggestion of more to do for her than I am doing. Dr. Peterson in New York told me he had a patient with similar reactions and there was a new drug he used that pulled her through. I have called here and there, trying to locate the drug. I finally found it in Atlanta, they are flying it in, by special plane, and the police will be at the airport to pick it up and rush it to the hospital as soon as it arrives. That and prayer is our last hope."

Tacky's Pastor, walked over, put his arms around Dr. Gross and said, "Doctor, I'm sorry. I misjudged you. I thought you were not doing anything for Tacky. Please forgive me."

With tears in his eyes, Dr. Gross said, "I can understand why. However, I do take my patients seriously, and I am doing everything in my power for Mrs. Knox. So far, nothing has seemed to help."

Tacky heard them talking faintly, as if they were far away. She couldn't see. Everything was in darkness, and her body felt as if it were floating in midair, moving farther and farther away on a long journey.

Tacky

Her life was holding on only by a thread, as her doctor, husband, and pastor stood helplessly by and prayed for the drug to arrive in time.

The police finally arrived with the new medication, and Dr. Gross injected it into the glucose drip running into Tacky's vein. A few hours later, more color appeared in Tacky's cheeks. Her breathing became less shallow and her pulse was stronger.

"These are good signs," Dr. Gross said hopefully.

Tacky remembered feeling as if her body were being pulled back to the hospital bed. Soon afterward, she saw a little light and heard faint voices. Her strength slowly returned until she was able to focus on objects again.

Cran stooped over her bed to kiss her gently. "Tacky, it's a relief to see you open your eyes again. I love you very much."

Smiling weakly, she tried to squeeze his hand, but the movement was so slight, he wondered if he imagined it.

She was in and out of the hospital many times during those nine months. When her labor began, it stopped just after three hours.

One Saturday afternoon, Tacky had just showered, bathed the boys and was setting out clothes for them. Cran was mowing the yard when she heard him call. Eppy, who was closest to the door and had on all his clothes except his shirt, ran to listen, then ran back.

"Mother, Daddy wants a rag."

Tacky grabbed the first clean cloth she saw and ran outside. She heard Cran give an exclamation, then he hopped around the mower to turn it off. His shoe was cut through, and blood spurted from the bottom. She grabbed a towel and ran out.

He said, "Get back in the house, you don't need to see all this blood."

Tacky

    She ran back inside and told the boys to grab their clothes
and get in the back seat of the car. After she gathered her purse
and car keys, they helped Cran into the passenger seat.

    "Put all the pressure you can stand on your foot with the
towel to try to stop the bleeding," she said, starting the engine.

    He wanted her to stop at the service station where some of
the church men always hung around and get one of them to drive
him, but she refused to waste time and kept going. She turned on
her flashing lights, and when she reached a red light, she leaned
on the horn, checked for other cars, and drove right through. Cran
was losing blood fast.

    Cran said, "Honey, you're going to get us all killed!
You don't need to be going through this anyway!"

    "Neither do you!" She sped down the street.

    Cran was rushed into surgery before Tacky had time to fill
out any papers. It turned out that the lawnmower struck a brick
buried in the yard, and the blade broke off, cutting through
Cran's shoe and almost cutting his foot in half.

    He was allergic to penicillin so they couldn't use that to
keep the infection down. Ten days later, an infection burst
through his stitches, and he needed another operation.

    Tacky's time was past, but the baby wasn't ready to be born.
She kept having labor pains that were regular and three minutes
apart that lasted only two or three hours, then they stopped.

    Finally a month after her due date, Dr. Gross said, "We can't
wait any longer." He sent Tacky to the hospital, and found the
baby was positioned wrong. He had to turn the baby and take her.

    "You have a beautiful baby girl," He said finally.
She weighed eight pounds and thirteen ounces, and had long black
hair, but her birth was very hard on Tacky. She vomited all over
the labor room and all the way from the labor room to the delivery
room.

126

Tacky

After the baby was delivered, Dr. Gross worked for hours trying to stop Tacky's bleeding. When he finally succeeded, packing her with gauze to keep pressure on the area, she started vomiting again and ejected the packing.

The delivery nurse scolded, "You cut that out! Dr. Gross worked for hours trying to clot that blood, and you just undid everything."

"Please, Nurse," Dr. Gross said. "She has vomited for ten months and can't help it."

He repeated placing pressure on Tacky's stomach and sides to stop the bleeding.

When Tacky could finally be moved to her own room, Cran came in, beaming. "OH, Honey we have the most beautiful baby girl you ever saw. She's got dark hair, a big roll on top and one on each side, with a little bow in the top. She's got fat rosy cheeks and looks two or three months old. She's so pretty!" He couldn't rave about his daughter enough.

Tacky, too weak to reply, smiled and thanked God for blessing them with a healthy baby girl, who they named Margo. She made their home complete.

"Isn't God wonderful?" she whispered, "Two fine sons and now a lovely baby girl. He is so good."

"He sure is. I can't wait to go tell the boys, Grandma, and all our friends." Cran beamed. He squeezed her hand, stooped, and kissed her. "The doctor wants you to get some much needed rest and wants me to get out of here. I'll be back a little later." She was already drifting off to sleep; she was so weak and worn out from the hard delivery. But so happy!

Tacky

CHAPTER SEVENTEEN

Tacky enjoyed sewing ruffled dresses and panties for Margo, then dressing her like a little doll. Her Daddy and the boys loved showing her off. People made a fuss over Eppy because of his playing and singing, and over Margo for being the only girl and baby, so Mike felt left out. He began showing off to get more attention.

One day, he was turning flips, and Tacky said, "You're just Mommy's little acrobat."

Eppy said, "You mean, Mommy's little acting brat." He didn't particularly enjoy Mike's mischief.

Tacky's health problems continued. She had several more breast surgeries for tumors. When Margo was three, Tacky needed a complete hysterectomy due to tumors.

"Oh Cran, I'm so sorry I keep having so much trouble and making it hard on you and the children," Tacky cried. "You might've been able to accomplish something if you had never married me."

"Don't ever let me hear you say that again. You are the best thing that ever happened to me. You know I love you, and I had rather have you with all your problems, than anyone else in the whole world, even if she never had health trouble." Cran said as he came over and comforted Tacky.

Lord, sometimes I get very discouraged, because I make life hard for my family, but You've blessed us so much, I'm ashamed when I feel sorry for myself. You give me the strength to do what I have to do, and I thank You for that. Just help me be the mother and wife my family needs, and help me teach our children to love and serve You.

Tacky was in the hospital a month after the hysterectomy, because she'd been hemorrhaging badly ever since Margo was born, and her health was poor. When she was finally able to return home, Mike was so thrilled that mother was coming home he rode his bicycle to the house next door to tell them his mother was home. Then he decided to aggravate Mrs. Moore, by riding around her house, blowing his bicycle horn. He rode away as fast as he could, looking back to see if she came out to scold him, and ran off the end of a culvert and into the bank.

He couldn't get up and screamed in pain. Tony, Mrs. Moore's adult son, ran over and picked him up to carry him home. Tacky had Mike placed on the bed beside her.

Every time any part of his body was moved, though, he screamed in pain. Tacky called Cran home from work, and he took Mike to the emergency room.

Margo and Mike were very close. As Cran left to take the boy to the hospital, Margo became hysterical.

Tacky called her to her bedside and put an arm around her. "Honey, we must trust God to take care of Mike. See, Mommy got to come home and God will take care of Mike, too."

Margo took a quick breath and said, "He will, won't He, Mommy?" Then she crawled up in the bed beside Tacky and went to sleep.

Tacky

It was difficult for Tacky to keep a positive attitude. So
many things had gone wrong for her and her family. She felt so
sorry for Cran. Whenever someone in his family was ill or hurt,
he felt it deeply. He was glad to finally have his wife home from
the hospital, only to have Mike become injured.

When he returned home, Cran looked so drawn. "He's got a
broken neck," he told Tacky. "The doctors said to keep him
stabilized and quiet. If we do, he should heal without being
paralyzed."

Although Mike healed as predicted, he always had stooped
shoulders afterward. Tacky often reminded him to stand up
straight, but the doctors told her he couldn't due to damage to
his cervical vertebras.

Tacky's health improved after the hysterectomy, and she
went to work when all the children were in school. Then another
tumor appeared in her breast, so she needed another operation. It
was the beginning of cancer, so Dr. Moore performed a bilateral
mastectomy.

One Saturday in February, 1961, while Tacky cooked for
Sunday, Eppy practiced the song he was going to play for the
brotherhood meeting that night. His daddy was president, and he
often took Eppy along to play and sing for them.

He played and sang, *He Lives*, then walked into the kitchen,
then walked into the kitchen. "Mother, just listen to those words:
You ask me how I know He lives, He lives within my heart.

That night, as he finished the song at the brotherhood
meeting, he fell to his knees beside the piano stool, and asked
Jesus to come into his heart. Cran and Tacky were thrilled.

On February 2, 1961, at a church Service, Michael gave his
heart to the Lord, and that was another glorious celebration.
Cran remarked often that he hoped the good Lord would let him live
long enough to see all his children saved.

130

One week later, on February ninth, Margo accepted the Lord as her Savior. Cran and Tacky were elated to have their whole family in the family of God.

In August,1961, Cran and Tacky took the children to town to buy their school clothes. To save time Tacky took Margo with her, and Cran took the boys. They let the children pick out the clothes they liked, but Margo couldn't make up her mind between two sets of three dresses. Tacky kept making suggestions, but she wanted Daddy to help her decide.

About that time Cran and the boys came in. She modeled the dresses for him, and wanted him to tell her which were the prettiest.

"You look so pretty in all of them, why don't we just buy all six." Cran said. That settled the question for Margo.

Tacky said, "You little con artist, your Daddy's spoiling you rotten." She just smiled and took her Daddy's hand, hugging him tightly.

Over time, Cran seemed depressed occasionally. He kept telling Tacky, "Something's going to happen. I don't know what or when, but somehow, I know I won't be here long."

"Please don't say that. How in the world would the children and I get by without you?" Tacky cried.

"You could make it much better without me than I would without you. You have stronger faith." Cran said as he hugged Tacky.

He took his vacation the week before school began and took the family to Jacksonville, Florida, renting a house on the beach with a boathouse set on pilings in the water. It was nice relaxing out there and reading while the children and Cran fished out the windows or off the pier. Cran did most of the cooking while there to allow Tacky to relax and gain strength.

"I want this to be the ideal vacation. I want you to

rest and relax and just thoroughly enjoy this trip, for I
feel that it will be the last we will ever have together,"
he told Tacky.

"Oh Cran, pleae don't talk like that." Tacky cried.

The children always enjoyed Daddy's cooking, for he got
something special to fix. Of course Tacky couldn't get something
special every day, so his cooking was a great treat for all the
family.

When they got back home, school began, and Cran was working
second shift at the plant. Each morning he got up early, took
Mike and Margo to school where he was using County equipment to
build a ball field for the children.

He scraped and leveled off a small hill, making a beautiful
ball field. He hauled in topsoil and sowed it with grass. He was
so excited to get it all fixed up. It would be ready for play
next spring when the baseball season began. The excess dirt was
leveled off down below the field.

When Tacky awoke Friday morning, September first, 1961, it
was raining. She cooked breakfast and told the children they
would have to ride the bus, because Daddy wouldn't be able to work
at school that day due to the rain. Besides, he desperately needed
a rest.

After getting the kids off to school, she straightened the
house and prepared for work, then went into the bedroom.

"Honey, it's raining. You can turn over and go back to sleep.
I'm going to work and the children have caught the bus for
school." She stooped over and kissed him.

"I'll stay in bed this morning, he agreed. I've never felt so
tired before. If you need me, just call. I love you." He said as
he tenderly touched her face.

"I love you, too, and I want you to rest. You
can't hold up with all the extra work you've been doing."

"I know, but I finished that beautiful ball field for the kids, and I'm proud of it. Now they can play at their own school."

Mike was the baseball player in the family. He pitched for his team and did very well. His Daddy worked with him, training him as much as possible.

Tacky was still trying to catch up on paperwork at the office since she was on vacation. She brought a sandwich and worked right through her lunch hour.

Just as she finished eating, Mama called.

"Tacky, call an ambulance and come home quick!" Mama whispered, barely able to talk.

"What's wrong, Mama?"

"Just call an ambulance and come quick!"

"You have to tell me what's wrong."

"I'm afraid Cran's been killed."

Tacky's boss, overhearing the conversation, came to Tacky's office. "What's wrong?"

Tacky, looking white, slowly hung up. "Mama said she was afraid Cran was killed. She...wants me to call an ambulance." She burst into tears.

Major immediately called an ambulance, then called Joe from the back room to drive Tacky home.

When they arrived at the house, they found a large crowd waiting in the yard. Tacky jumped out of the car and ran toward the house, but someone held her back.

"Please don't go there."

"I've got to see what happened!" Tacky said, tearing herself loose.

The beautiful oak tree in their side yard was smoking, and Cran lay in the branches, one leg and arm dangling down.

Paramedics and a doctor were waiting to administer first aid as soon as Cran was brought down, but Tacky knew it was too late.

As she gazed at the tree, she remembered Psalms 46:1, *The Lord is my refuge and strength, a very present help in trouble.*

It was clear Cran had been trimming the tree. He worried about it often. When wind came, branches rubbed against the telephone line, sending up sparks, and he feared the children might be playing out there someday and receive a lethal shock, especially after a rain.

Tacky had called both the Power Company and the Telephone Company. They promised to look into the situation and trim back the tree branches, but had never got to it. While on vacation, Cran worried about the tree and declared he'd trim it if someone else didn't do it soon.

When the sun came out at ten o'clock that morning, he got up and started trimming the trees in the yard. Tacky thought, *Cran lost his life trying to protect the family he loved.*

Tacky allowed someone to take her by the arm and lead her inside the house, where she sank down on a couch, too exhausted to breathe.

Someone suggested going to school to pick up Mike and Margo. Tacky looked at her watch, "Please don't bring them home until Cran's body is removed from the tree. I don't want the children to remember such a terrible sight."

Eppy was in Junior High School across town in Attalla. She felt sure Cran's body would be gone before he got home, because the bus took a very long route.

It seemed like a nightmare. She remembered Cran telling her something was about to happen. He, the one who was always healthy except for one bout of spinal meningitis, had been killed. How in

the world would she ever manage without him?. He was a staunch
husband and father during her many hospital confinements.

Tacky slowly went to the phone to call Todd, her brother, who
lived in Arizona. They'd always been close. Todd would want to
be one of the first to know.

"Sis, we'll be there as fast as we can," he promised.

"Don't come back. You were here just a few weeks ago, and I
know you can't afford another trip. There's nothing you can do."

"We'll be there as fast as as our little Volkswagon can make
it."

Tacky's legs knotted up with cramps. She rubbed, walked,
cried, and did everything she could to work them out. Friends
rubbed her feet and calves on both legs, trying to ease the cramps
without success.

Finally someone called Dr. Gross, who said to get a
dishpan of hot water and another of cold water and transfer the
feet from one to the other. That finally worked. Tacky walked the
floor with leg cramps when she was pregnant, but she never felt
anything like that before. Dr. Gross said it was probably brought
on due to shock.

CHAPTER EIGHTEEN

After the funeral and the graveside Scripture and prayer,
the pastor and friends gave their condolences, then the
funeral director asked the family to leave until they lowered the
casket, covered the grave, and arranged the flowers.

Tacky and the children went back to the car to wait. It
drizzled that day, but friends came to the car to shake Tacky's
hand and share the family's grief. When another hand came through
the window, she took it without looking. When a squeeze and caress
began, she looked up and saw a drunk outside, staggering and
caressing her while he winked.

Tacky jerked her hand free, raised the window, and locked the
door. Her husband was hardly cold in the grave when that man
insulted her, and she began to cry. Margo snuggled close to her,
and Eppy and Mike patted her shoulders from the back seat.

Tacky tried to control herself. *Don't be hard on him,* she
told herself. *He's so drunk, he doesn't know what he's doing.*
A sense of pity replaced the sense of complete revulsion.

Tacky stayed home for one week after the funeral to take care
of all the details following her husband's death.

One Saturday Margo came in from playing and put her arms

around Tacky's neck, and said, "Mommy, I miss Daddy so much.
Just think I only had a daddy for seven years."

Tacky hugged her tightly. "Yes, Honey, I know you do. We all
miss him, but think how fortunate you were to have such a
wonderful daddy for seven whole years. Many children never see
their daddy, and some are treated so badly by their fathers,
they'd be glad if they left. You had a wonderful friend and daddy.
You've been a blessed little girl!"

Mike called Margo to come play with him. She hugged
her mother's neck and said, "I guess so, for Daddy was wonderful
to all of us." Then she ran out to play.

Tears filled Tacky's eyes as she went about her work.
It was so hard to be brave for the children, and strive to
make things as normal as possible. The hardest time, for
Tacky, was after the children were tucked in at night. Many
times she would think she heard Cran call from the kitchen
door..."*Honey, I'm home.*" And she would jump out of bed, and
be almost to the door before she realized it was only a dream.
The nights were so long and lonely. It had been such a comfort to
snuggle up to Cran's big, strong, warm, body. Tacky seemed always
to be cold, but Cran's body was always so warm and cozy, and she
felt so secure in his strong arms.

She tried hard to be thankful for the fifteen years they
had together, and not feel sorry for herself and the children.
She knew God had really blessed them, but that didn't do away with
that intense loneliness. She tried to bury herself in her work
and in the children's activities. But many nights were filled with
such intense loneliness that Tacky cried herself into a fitful,
exhausted sleep. She hadn't realized just how much she had come
to depend on Cran's strength. When she was unable to do the many
things that a home required, he always filled in, and now they all
missed him so much.

Tacky

Everything began happening after the funeral. The oven unit
burned out on the stove. Tacky purchased one and replaced it
herself; then, the fan motor burned out on the Maytag Freezer.
She couldn't get it to work and finally had to call a repairman.

Eppy's face broke out in a big, red rash with spots and his
eyes became infected. Tacky took him to Dr. Gross. He said it
was caused from shock, and gave him some nerve medication. Tacky
had physical problems that were new, too, which Dr. Gross also
said came from shock.

A little boy stuck a pencil in Mike's hand as they waited for
the school bus. He tried to stab Mike's chest, but he threw up
his hand and caught it. When Tacky came in from work, Mike's hand
was swollen and angry looking. She had him soak it in warm salt
water, and picked pieces of pencil lead out of it.

The next day when he came in it was swollen worse and his
little finger was curling inward, while red streaks ran up his
arm. Tacky called Dr. Gross and took Mike in immediately. Dr.
Gross froze the wound, opened it, and removed more pieces of
pencil lead. He cleaned out the area, sewed it up, and said he
thought it would be all right.

About a week later when Mike came in from school, his hand
was swollen with red streaks running up his arm again. Tacky
called the doctor again. An x-ray revealed a long piece of pencil
lead had worked between the finger bones, ligaments and muscles in
his hand. He said it would be such a delicate surgery to get it
out without injuring the muscles and ligaments that he would have
to put him in the hospital and put him to sleep.

Mike also had some other difficulties with his gonads, which
Tacky worried about, so Dr. Gross said he'd perform both
operations while the boy was completely unconscious.

If Cran were only here, Tacky thought.

138

Michael recovered well after the surgery. He was in a lot of pain at first, but he was able to return home after only three days. Mrs. Moore, their neighbor, brought him some frozen strawberries, that certainly made him feel better. After Thanksgiving, Mike returned to school.

Then the well pump began giving trouble. It would not hold a prime, and every night after supper, Mama and Tacky would have to go outside and work on it. One night at eleven o'clock, they were almost frozen in the cold weather when the pump was finally repaired.

Mama walked around it and stubbed her toe on it. Something broke, sending water everywhere, covering both women. Mama was so shocked, she just stood there stuttering as they were both sprayed with water.

Tacky began laughing. Mama said, "I'm so sorry. I couldn't help it. But I sure don't see anything funny about it."

"Mama, if you could only see your face. Anyway, it was either laugh or cry. Neither of us needed any more tears." She began the tedious process of repairing the new damage .

Finally, after several weeks of priming the pump every night, they pulled the hose from the well and found gravel lodged in the foot valve.

Tacky thanked the Lord she always helped Cran with repairs around the house and had some idea what to do. She was determined not to be a widow who depended on friends and relatives to do all her repairs.

Mike played ball on the Farm Team and in Little League. After every game, he asked, "Mother are you coming to my next game?"

"As long as I can sit up, I'll be at your games." Tacky promised.

It kept her very busy. Eppy took music and played in the school band. Margo was in the Church Girl's Auxiliary Program, of which Tacky was the leader.

Peter Knox told her one day, "Tacky, you're killing yourself running with your children to keep them in so many activities. There just isn't any sense in it."
He and Teresa only had one son, but he wasn't active in any of the extra school or church functions.

Tacky said, "Well, Peter, I had rather wear myself out keeping them in worthwhile activities than wear myself out trying to get them out of something bad they've done because they weren't busy."

Cran's brother had a stroke while living in another state. The family was so worn from sitting around the clock with him that Tacky went two week-ends to relieve some members of the family. She and a nurse were turning him to put a light on a bed sore to try to dry it up, when she felt something pull in the back of her neck. She began having terrible headaches that no amount of pain reliever would ease. She was in and out of the hospital for tests and medication. Nothing seemed to do any good, except traction. As long as her head was in traction with eight to ten pound weights pulling on it, she felt some relief, but couldn't stay in traction the rest of her life.

Margo became so nervous and hysterical every time Tacky had to go into the hospital that she did everything to prevent surgery. Margo felt that she wouldn't have a daddy or mother if she had surgery.

The pain became unbearable after three years of intense suffering, so Tacky went to Birmingham to a Neurosurgeon. He did a milligram test and discovered a ruptured disk in her cervical spine.

"You've been in a car wreck," he said.

Tacky, said, "No, when I helped a nurse turn a patient, I felt something pull, and the pain began."

"I know, but nothing could splatter a disk like that except being hit from behind in a car wreck. This happened several years before. When you helped that nurse, you embedded the spurs that had formed around the ruptured disk into the nerves. That's what caused the headaches."

Tacky remembered driving down the mountain to the hospital to sit with Uncle Arthur while Aunt Mary had surgery several years before. A neighbor was driving without brakes for two days and stripped his transmission gears trying to slow down, hitting her from behind. She was unable to turn her head for weeks afterward. The doctors had diagnosed it as neuritis, myacitis, arthritis, spastic muscles and inflamed nerves.

The neurosurgeon explained the pros and cons. "If we don't do surgery, and do it soon, your right arm will be paralyzed. Your brain cannot take the pressure put on it continuously without it snapping. However, if we do surgery, it is in such a strategic area that you could be paralyzed the rest of your life, or you might become an imbecile. I guess you would like to go home, talk it over with your family before you decide."

Tacky said, "No. I don't want my family to know how serious this is. I've gone as long as I can stand already. Should the Lord see fit for any of the bad things you mentioned, then He'll find someone to care for my children. He's taken me through twenty-odd surgeries before, and He can get me through this. Schedule it as soon as possible."

He patted her shoulder. "If you feel that way about it, I know you'll come out fine."

After the surgery, he came out looking for some of Tacky's family. "Is anyone here with Mrs. Lula Knox?" He asked.

Eppy jumped up, "I'm her son."

The surgeon looked at him and said, "I don't believe a word
of it. She's too young to have a son your age."

Eppy laughed. "Tell her that when she wakes up."

When Tacky awoke after the surgery, her doctor was by her
bedside. He asked her to move her fingers, then her toes.When she
was able to do both, he patted her on the shoulder and said.

"That's fine. I knew you were going to be all right. By the
way, there's a fine-looking young man in the waiting room who
claims to be your son, but that can't be right. You're too young
to have a son that age."

Tacky smiled. "Oh, he's mine all right."

Tacky was very proud of her three children. Etheridge
was just like his father. He was growing fast and his musical
talent was developing as rapidly as his body. He was choir
director for a Baptist Church in South Gadsden and doing a good
job at it.

Tacky beamed whenever someone mentioned her children. Mike
was still pitching for the Little League, and Margo was playing
the accordion and using it in her Girl's Auxiliary work when they
visited shut-ins.

The children were all so different, but each had his or her
own individual talent, making the diversity at home interesting.

Etheridge was drum Major for the marching band at Etowah
High School. He played clarinet or whatever the band needed for a
concert. He graduated from high school and immediately enrolled at
Auburn University. He worked his way through school by playing
music.

During his last year in college, he received an opportunity
through his music to go to South America. His teachers let him
take his finals a few days early so he could make the trip. He was
away for six months, playing and singing, and enjoying the

beautiful Amazon and the ruggedness of the South American scenery.
He returned home to follow a career in music.

Temple and Son Electric, where Tacky worked, had branched out
opening an office in Decatur, Alabama and wanted Tacky to transfer
with the company as Office Manager in the new location.

It was a hard decision to make. To pull up stakes and leave
their home and all their friends would be hard for all of them.
Tacky prayed fervently that God would help her make the right
decision.

Michael had begun to skip school some and that bothered
Tacky tremendously. After much prayer she felt led to move.
Michael didn't want to leave Gadsden.

After Cran's death, Tacky had told the children, "I can't be
at home with you all the time, I have to work to help make a
living. Grandmother will be with you, but you have a tendency to
talk her into anything you want to do. So anytime you leave the
house you are to call and get permission from me. I have to be
away during the day, but I want to know where you are and what
you're doing at all times. If you try otherwise, I will have you
put in reform school, rather than worry about your being in
trouble."

When Tacky announced the decision to move, Michael was very
upset. He didn't want to leave his friends.

Margo said, "Mike, just think, we'll still have our friends
here and make new ones up there. That'll even be more friends."

Michael didn't see it that way and grumbled and growled
about it. This hurt Tacky tremendously, but she knew she had
to make the decisions for her family and was convinced the
Lord was leading in the move.

"Son, I'm sorry you feel that way, but I've prayed about this
move for weeks and feel that it is the right thing to do."

He pouted about the change and wouldn't have anything to

Tacky

do with the boys that visited him when they moved into Priceville,
a suburb of Decatur. One night after some neighbors had left,
Tacky was talking with him about being so cold and unfriendly.

"I'd rather go to reform school as to live here." He said.

Tacky had to be firm. She said, "Michael, there's a
correctional school on 31 South for boys; if you feel that's where
you need to be, then I guess I will just have to put you there. I
have to make a living and I need your cooperation. If I can't
depend on that, I'll just have to work something else out. We're
here to stay because I can earn more for my family. I love you
and wish the situation were different, but it isn't. We have to
make the best of it."

Gradually, Michael accepted the friendship of others and
became involved in community affairs. Tacky was very relieved.

Slowly, signs of joy and happiness came to her children's
lives.

Tacky heard about a family who needed help in which the
husband and father was dying of lead poisoning. She and Janie from
church went to visit them. They didn't have water in their shack,
and everything was dirty. The house had a bad odor.

Tacky and Janie told the family they'd return the following day
to take their dirty clothes to a laundromat for cleaning. They
took bedclothes, towels, curtains, and anything washable in the
house.

After all day, using every washer and dryer, they returned
with clean, folded clothes. Some of the church men hauled water
to the house for them, and they scrubbed the floors. Tacky
brought the mother and daughters home with her to clean them up
and let Margo cut their hair.

Janie took the boys home with her, and cut their hair, and
had them wash in her bathtub.

Tacky was cleaning up the bathroom with lysol when Mike

came in. The smell from their visitors was still noticeable.

"Mother, what in the world do you mean bringing such trash into our home?" He asked. "Letting them use our bathtub. Do you want to give us some kind of disease? The whole house stinks!"

"Mike, just hush," Tacky scolded. "I'll spray the house and get rid of that odor after I take them back home. I'll scrub everything with Lysol to disinfect it, too. We are trying to help this family, and if we can clean them up and get them in church, maybe we can teach them to help themselves. You just need to be thankful that you have a clean home to live in and have more compassion for people who aren't as fortunate as we are!"

The family did come to Church for awhile, but only one of the daughters continued coming. The father passed away and the family moved away. But the younger daughter continued in church and elevated her life by keeping clean. She married and raised some fine daughters of her own.

Tacky had great compassion on sick and unfortunate people. In 1972, when a tornado came through Priceville and destroyed many homes and property, Tacky took casseroles, strawberries, and cakes, and other foods to many of the people who'd been affected by the disaster. She loved to prepare meals for others when they needed them.

She said, "The Good Lord has blessed me with help every time I was in a situation where I couldn't provide for myself, and I am only trying to serve Him by passing on some of the blessings I have received."

Michael graduated from high school with honors, but he Still considered Gadsden as the perfect place to live. He announced he was moving back whether anyone wanted to come with him or not. Tacky thought he was too young to be turned loose on his own, and she felt disheartened with her job. many promises made to her hadn't come through.

She returned to Gadsden, found another job, and made as much as she made before after working for one company ten years. After asking the renters who were in her house to move, she moved her family back.

Michael soon saw that Gadsden wasn't as perfect as he thought. He fell in love with a girl in Priceville and couldn't wait to get back to Decatur. He got a job at 3M, found an apartment, and saw that being on his own wasn't as much fun as he thought, either.

"Mother, when will you move back to Priceville?" he asked. "I I didn't realize I had it so good at home. I never thought about the blessing of coming in from work to food on the table, a clean bed, a clean house, and clean clothes. I didn't realize until I was living on my own how much work that is."

"We're here because of you, Michael," she said. "We can't run from one city to another. It costs money to move, besides all the hard work."

"I know, but I have learned my lesson. I sure wish you'd move back. I'll rent a moving van and get my friends to help. Margo and I can do all the packing."

Margo said, "Mother, that could be our Christmas present. That's all we'll ask for Christmas if you'll just move back."

Mama wasn't happy in Gadsden, and neither were the children. That bothered Tacky. She prayed about the move, then spoke with her boss.

"No one's happy here, and I feel that I will find work up there before we go hungry. God has always provided, I believe He'll do it again."

Her boss was very understanding. She trained her replacement and prepared to move once again.

They moved on Christmas Eve. Tacky stopped about five miles

from home to get gas, and a friend told her, "Mrs. Knox, I think I know where you can get a job if you are interested."

"Where?   I am certainly interested."

"I was talking with Mr. Johnson at General Construction. He said for you to call him after Christmas if you were interested."

Tacky got the man's name and number and called the day after Christmas and set up an appointment for an interview.   She got the job.   Then, she went back to Gadsden and closed out her books for the year and began work on her new job on January second.

She was very excited, and she didn't even miss a day of work.

God is so good to us, she mused

One night, Michael spoke with Tacky and said, "Mother, I have a confession to make.   I didn't want to move from Gadsden the first time because the boys I was running around with were so close.   We were skipping school and getting into minor things that would've led to bigger things if I stayed.   I doubt I would've even graduated from high school.   I certainly would've been in trouble a lot."

Tacky said, "Michael, I prayed fervently for God's guidance, and I didn't know why He guided me away, except that I thought it might be because of the increase in salary.   When I knew you were against moving it was hard to be firm and move anyway, but God gave me the strength to do it.   Isn't He wonderful to us?"

CHAPTER NINETEEN

Michael worked for a short time at 3M, then went into
the Army. He wanted to get married, and wanted his service
in the armed forces over first.

After basic training he was sent to Fort Rucker, Georgia, in
the mechanic's division. They told him he could stay and teach
mechanics instead of going to Vietnam, but he wanted to get out of
the service as quickly as possible, so he went to Vietnam.

May 27, 1971, Tacky drove home from work and thought over the
past ten years since Cran was killed. *God has been so good to us.*
In two more days, Margo will finish high school, then she'll
finish the cosmetology course she began last summer. She wants to
marry the young man she's madly in love with.

Mike will finish his term of service and soon be able to
return to his beloved. Etheridge is following a musical career.
Soon, all the children will be on their own, and I can quit the
extra bookkeeping job I have in the evenings. I won't have to make
ends meet like before. Things are looking up.

Margo was out of school for the last two days because of
senior privilege. She drove Grandma to Collinsville, seventy-five
miles away to go to her twin grandsons' graduation. Margo came

back through Gadsden to visit the school she attended before moving to Decatur. It was so good to see her friends again.

Tacky walked in whistling and humming, "To God Be The Glory, Great Things He Hath Done," as she began preparing supper for her and Margo, who'd be in very soon. Even the rain didn't dampen her spirits today.

The telephone rang, and she answered. "Hello?"

"This is Hartselle Hospital. Do you know a young girl named Margo Knox?"

"I do," Tacky said, feeling apprehensive.

"She's been in a car wreck, and we're trying to locate her mother."

"How bad is it?"

"She's critical. Do you know how to contact her mother?"

"I am her mother," Tacky whispered.

"I'm so sorry. Please forgive me for being so blunt. Can you come here immediately?"

"Yes, I'll be right there."

She turned the power off the stove, grabbed her coat, purse, and keys and ran from the house. As she got into the car, she thought, *I'd better let someone know where I'm going.*

She pulled into her neighbor's driveway and ran inside to tell them the news.

"Mandy said , "I'm going with you." She grabbed a coat and keys. "We'll go in my car."

When they arrived at the hospital a nurse took them to an office, where a doctor was on the phone. "Dr. French will be with you shortly." the nurse said.

"Maybe this is the young lady's mother," the doctor said into the phone. "If so, she'll be on her way immediately." He hung up and looked at her, "Mrs. Knox?"

"Yes. How's my daughter?"

Tacky

"I hate to have to tell you this, but your daughter's in very critical condition. She has a broken neck and back, all her ribs are broken on one side and three on the other, and they are torn loose from the sternum. T-4 and T-5 in her spine are completely crushed and her spinal chord is severed, paralyzing her from the T-4 Vertebrae down, which is midway in the back. We're sending her to Birmingham to the University Medical Center. I've already contacted the best neurologist in the country for her."

Tacky felt as though all the wind had been knocked out of her with this news.

"If you're ready to go, I have an ambulance waiting to take her." He patted Tacky on the shoulder.

"I'll go back and call our pastor, and we'll bring your car down." Mandy said. "What about clothes?"

"I left my keys in the car which has my house keys on it. You'll find a suitcase in my bedroom closet already packed with underclothes, toothbrush and etc. I always keep one packed for emergencies. Just look in the closet and get whatever clothes you think I will need and put them in the hanging bag you will find there. I appreciate this, Mandy." Hugging her friend, she went down to ride in the ambulance with Margo.

The eighty-mile ambulance drive was a nightmare. Margo was strapped to the ambulance cot, but kept trying to come up off it. Tacky and the assistant worked and talked trying to keep her still. Delirious, Margo wanted to get up. Once, she thought it was her boyfriend holding her down. The next time, she thought it was her brother. She fought with all she had to get up off that gurney.

It was raining hard, and people sometimes wouldn't pull over for the ambulance. The driver had to use his loudspeaker more than

once, shouting, "WILL YOU PLEASE PULL OVER!" to get people's
attention.

Tacky was so thankful when they finally arrived at the
hospital.

Etheridge had an apartment in Birmingham, and Tacky called
Him, but he wasn't in. When Mandy and Tacky's pastor
came in, he took down the address and went to see where Etheridge
was. He left a message on the young man's door, but he was
playing music out of town and didn't return home for many hours.

Etheridge immediately rushed to the hospital. A team of
neurosurgeons and orthopedic surgeons discussed Margo's condition.
They took x-rays and ran tests all day Friday, then scheduled
surgery for Saturday at seven o'clock in the morning.

Etheridge was a close friend of one of the head nurses. She
told him that Doc Adams of *Gunsmoke* just had open-heart surgery at
the hospital a few weeks earlier, and Margo was getting more
attention than he had. She had never seen the doctors so
concerned about a patient.

On Saturday morning, there were so many friends from Gadsden
and Decatur coming to the hospital, the entire group had to be
moved to the dining area to wait.

The neurosurgeon began surgery at seven o'clock and finished
at two. He said, "T-4 and T-5 were crushed and splintered and the
spinal cord was severed with jagged edges. We carefully removed
all the crushed and splintered bone, trimmed the edges of the
spinal cord, and sewed it back together, packed it in jelly, and
turned her over to the orthopedic surgeons."

The orthopedic surgeons finished at seven o'clock that
evening. "We removed bone from Margo's hip and fused the spine
back together, then put large pins on each side of the spine and
placed her on a Strike-0-Frame, which has bars webbed with bands
fastened to a frame. She'll lie on her back for an hour. and

they'll put another set of bars over her and fasten them together,
then turn her so she'll be face down for an hour. She has to be
turned every hour, day or night. She can't stay in a bed for six
weeks."

There was so much pressure on Margo's chin when she was
flipped on her stomach, it gave her intense pain. Etheridge
adjusted the straps and had the nurse bring a baby diaper to
support her chin. Finally, they found a position that was
comfortable.

A few days after the surgery, Margo began asking questions.
"Why can't I move my legs? Are they broken?"

The doctor sat down with her and said, "I'm sorry, but you're
paralyzed."

"For how long?" she asked.

He said, "Honey, I hate to tell you this but it will be for
life, unless there is a miracle."

She just said, "Well, I have use of my mind and arms and
hands, I guess I'll just have to get by without my legs."

After the doctor left, Etheridge asked her, "Margo, do you
understand what the doctor said?"

"Yes, he said I was paralyzed."

"But do you understand what that means?"

"It means I'll never walk again."

Tacky prayed that God would help her during that terrible
time. Margo had always been an active child. Anything the boys
did, she tried to do better. She taught trampoline at school,
something she had a flair for. She was an expert swimmer and
excelled in many other sports, and she'd been a cheerleader. How
would she adjust to life in a wheelchair?

"It means you'll be in a wheelchair the rest of your life,
Sis," Etheridge said. "Do you really understand."

Margo finally broke down and cried. Tacky and Etheridge

cried with her. But after she cried it out, she adjusted to the trauma by making up her mind that life had to go on and she would just have to make the best of it.

Tacky was proud of her, but she knew Margo had a lot to learn. There were many adjustments, filled with pain and heartache, waiting for her.

"Lord, Tacky prayed, please be with us and give me strength, wisdom, and guidance in working with her through these trials. If there hadn't been so many other things before this in my life, I'd say it was impossible for me to handle this, but You made the impossible become possible before, and I know You can do it again. Thank You for Your strength and guidance. Amen.

CHAPTER TWENTY

Margo was in the hospital for four months, she had learned to exercise on a mat on the floor, and tried to learn to walk on crutches even though she was paralyzed from her chest down. She fell often, and her thigh had became swollen and red. The muscles in it had become hard.

Several doctors began checking it. Her body was depositing calcium into the muscle and changing it to bone. Only one of the thirty-odd doctors who saw her had ever heard of something like it. X-rays were taken each day as the doctors wondered what to do.

Margo had been under a lot of radiation treatments since the accident. and no one knew the answer to this calcium deposit problem, so they told her to continue exercising and building up her strength until they could decide what to do.

Some of the neighbors had been working with the Red Cross to get Mike home from Vietnam and help Tacky when Margo finally came home. The medical bills were becoming insurmountable.

When Mike arrived, he was shocked to find his always-so-active sister in such a tragic condition. She used to leg wrestle her brother, and she always threw him. When they moved to Decatur,

Tacky

he was determined to find someone that could throw her, so he
invited the strongest boys in his house to challenge her. But no
one could throw her.

They lay on their backs in opposite directions and
raised their adjoining legs. On the count of three, they locked
their legs and tried to flip each other. Margo always won,
something that always bugged Mike.

Looking at her now, knowing she couldn't move her legs at
all, was heartbreaking.

When he and Tacky were alone, Mike sked, "Mother, what in the
world will we do? How will we ever be able to meet our
obligations?"

Tacky put her arm around him. "I don't know, son. We may
have to sell our house to meet the bills, but she's doing much
better than the doctors expected. It could be worse. God has
always provided for us. He won't stop now."

"I know, Mom. Nothing's so bad that it couldn't be worse,
from the day we're born till we ride in a hearse." He grinned and
hugged her.

Dr. Stokes came in one Saturday when Tacky was with Margo and
asked, "Margo, what type of work do you plan to go into when
you're out of the hospital?"

"Cosmetology," She quickly replied.

"Honey, there is no way you can do that in a wheelchair."

"Dr. Stokes, I finished more than three hundred hours in that
field before the wreck, and I'm not about to give it up now."

"But Margo, you can't do it now. Why don't you become a
counselor or maybe a social worker? With your cheerful
disposition you'd do well in these fields," He reasoned.

"I don't want to be a counselor or social worker. I want to
be a hair dresser," she said emphatically.

"But Honey, if you can't do it, you can't do it. There's

just no way you can do that from a wheelchair."

"Then I'll find a way. I can do anything I did before.
I'll just have to learn new methods."

Dr. Stokes gave Tacky a pleading look. "Please talk
some sense into your daughter."

"Dr. Stokes, I wouldn't try to discourage her for anything.
Let her try. If she can't do it, she'll change her own mind."

"You're as stubborn as she is." He smiled, hugged her and
turned to walk out. At the door he turned and said, "We'll see
what we can work out."

The next evening when Tacky left for home, Dr. Stokes came
into the room. "Margo, you are so determined to pursue this
cosmetology field, we're sending you to the handicap school two-
and-a-half blocks up the street to show you that it can't be done
from a wheelchair. Beginning in the morning, you will get up, eat
breakfast, take your bath, dress, and wheel yourself to the school
by eight o'clock--without any help whatsoever."

Margo merely smiled, "I'll make it!"

"The way you like to sleep late, we'll see." He grinned.

Tacky could hardly wait until the following Saturday, when
she could see how Margo's schooling had worked out. Just as she
got on the elevator to go to Margo's room, Dr. Stokes stepped on.

"Good Morning, Dr. Stokes," she said. "How's Margo's
cosmetology course coming?"

"Don't mention Cosmetology to me." He grinned. "That
Margo, has been up, bathed, dressed, eaten breakfast and rolled
up there without help from anyone every morning, and the
instructor tells me there is no need for her to come back,
for she can already do more than they even teach there."

"Then, when she gets out of the hospital she can pursue
the cosmetology course?" Tacky enquired.

Tacky

"Well, it's going to be an awful hard field, but with her determination, what else can we do? That young lady really has spunk, and that's really what it takes to get anywhere with her handicap."

Dr. Stokes held the door while Tacky stepped off the elevator.

"Thanks," she said, smiling. "See you later." She hurried to Margo's room.

Margo smiled as her mother entered. "Guess what?" she asked eagerly.

"I know. Dr. Stokes rode in the elevator with me."

"Really? What did he have to say?" Margo asked.

"He's proud of you. He says it won't be easy, but you'll make it."

Margo grinned, "Changed his mind, didn't he?"

"Guess he had to after you showed him." Tacky laughed and stooped to hug Margo. "They'll find out that the Knox family aren't quitters."

Margo laughed, "Sure thing, Mom."

When word got out about Margo's decision, the doctors began teasing her. One bald doctor came in and said, "Miss Hairdresser, I'd like to get my hair cut, please."

Margo promptly pitched a pillow on the floor, took her scissors from a bedside drawer, and said, "Sit in my chair, please."

She picked her feet up with her hand, one at a time and pitched them across the bed and scooted where she could reach his bushy eyebrows, and began trimming them, as that was all the hair he had. When she had finished she handed him a hand mirror.

He smiled and said, "Why, that's the best haircut I've ever had."

Dr. Stokes was a timid doctor, but one Saturday he came in with some burgundy pants on, (his wife had purchased for him) under his long white jacket. Margo loved teasing him and said loudly,

"OOOOH WEEEE, just look at Dr. Stoke's RED PANTS!"

He blushed and turned to the other patient in the room without saying a word.

Soon the doctors decided to let Margo come home on weekends to see how she handled herself at home. Some of the neighbors built a wheelchair ramp and widened the bathroom door so she could get in. Maneuvering at home was more difficult than at the hospital, because houses weren't built for paraplegics.

Tacky had to fold towels over the door track on the bathtub, so Margo could sit down to get in and out of the tub, but before her next visit, she had a friend take a twenty-inch piece of two-by-six and cut grooves in it so it would sit firmly on the tracks to provide a stable seat.

Many similar adjustments were made to other parts of the house.

Dr. Stokes told Tacky before Margo came home on a visit, "It is very important that you allow Margo to do everything for herself. It might take thirty minutes for her to perform a task you could do in five, but you'll be harming her if you do it."

It wasn't easy to see Margo struggling with simple tasks at home, but she had to learn. After five-and-a-half months and many weekends at home, Margo was finally dismissed from the hospital.

She immediately called to set up an appointment to enter college to finish her courses. Since her first class used to be upstairs without an elevator, she transferred to Calhoun Junior College. A female instructor told her to come in to discuss her transfer.

When Tacky and Margo arrived, Mrs. Brown had stepped out. Mr. Roberts took one look at Margo and said, "There is no use waiting

Tacky

to talk with Mrs. Brown. There is no way you can go do school
here. You can't even get in and out of the building. Even if you
could do that, there's no way you could do the work.

"We'll have a ramp built for her to get in and out, if
The school will allow it." Tacky said.

"No. There's no way the work can be done from a wheelchair.
"But there is, Mr. Roberts." Margo argued.

"There is no way! You would be in the other students' way,
and they would be in your way. It can't be done."

Tacky rolled Margo's chair outside toward their car just as
Mrs. Brown drove up. Seeing tears in both their eyes, she asked,
"What's wrong?"

Margo replied, "Mr. Roberts won't even give me a chance to
prove what I can do."

"She's going to get a chance if we have to take it up with
higher officials!" Tacky's jaw was set.

Mrs. Brown saw Mr. Roberts standing in the doorway. "What
did you tell them, Mr. Roberts?"

"I said there was no way she could do someone's hair from her
chair, and there's no use wasting their time and ours."

"Now, Mr. Roberts, we can't say no without giving a student a
chance, can we?"

"Ordinarily, no, but she doesn't have any chance at all."

"Not unless we give it to her." Mrs. Brown replied.

"We'll build a ramp if you'll give us permission, Tacky said
quickly.

"Margo, be here Monday at eight. We'll help you in for the
first few days."

"Oh, thank you! Margo and Tacky exclaimed.

Mr. Roberts gave Mrs. Brown a nasty look, but she smiled
sweetly back at him.

Margo returned to school early Monday morning.

Tacky drove her there on the way to work and helped her inside.
Margo entered her studies with enthusiasm and determination. It
wasn't easy, and she was still weak from almost six months in the
hospital, but she put all her strength into it.

Since she would soon be working with the public, Margo had to
go to the Health Department for a tuberculosis inoculation. The
next day, Margo's arm was red, and she didn't feel very well. She
went to school but had chills all day. She refused to call Tacky
to come after her. Margo wanted her training so badly, she
would go through anything to get it.

That night Margo's temperature run very high, and she had
chills all night. The next day, she passed blood through her
catheter. Tacky called Dr. Stokes and took her back to
Birmingham. When the physical therapist learned she was coming in
for a check-up, she told Dr. Stokes to wear his burgundy pants.

He said, "I'll never be able to wear those pants again."

"Aw, Dr. Stokes. They look nice on you, and it would thrill
Margo to see you in them again."

"Nope, Never again, not even for Margo," he declared.

After checking Margo, he admitted her to the hospital to run
an IVP and other tests. He thought she just had kidney stones. He
told Tacky to return to work, because Margo needed tests for
several days. He promised to call when they knew something.

The following day, Dr. Stokes told the nurse to call Tacky
and ask her to return to the hospital.

Tacky went to Margo's room and found her crying. "Mother, I'm
pregnant. It isn't something that has been going on. It just
happened unexpectedly. I have always said I would never go to bed
with a man before marriage, but Rocky and I were planning to
get married right away, and it seemed so right. We talked about it
later and wondered why we went that far."

"Dr. Stokes and all the doctors here want me to have an

abortion. They say I've been under so much radiation there's
no way the baby will be normal." She began crying
uncontrollably.

Tacky hugged her tightly until she regained control.
Margo wiped her eyes and said, "Mother, they say it will be born
with half a face, a stump of an arm or leg or some other bad
deformity, but there is no way I can do away with my baby!"

The two women held each other and cried. Tacky was so
shocked, she didn't know what to say.

Margo said, "Mother, I'm truly sorry, I never intended to
hurt and dishonor you this way."

"Don't worry about that now, Margo. We must ask God for
guidance in this situation."

"Mother, this happened a week and a half before my accident
and the doctors say the shock of the accident should have
destroyed the baby. All the radiation I have been under from the
very beginning of conception should have dried it up. All the
falling I have done trying to walk, should have caused a
miscarriage. Then they argue that no one has ever had so much
kidney poison without a miscarriage. I believe the Lord has
protected my baby through all this, and I am not about to have an
abortion. They tell me I can have one and no one will ever know.
I want my baby more than anything in the world, and I was forgiven
of the sin long before I knew there was a baby on the way. I
don't care what people say, or think, I want my baby!"

"Margo, I don't know how we'll manage all this, either
financialy or physically, but God has provided a way for us
over the years, and I feel sure He will help us work this out
also. We'll just trust it to Him. Remember the song, *Little is
Much When God is in it?*"

Margo came home, and Tacky went by the Church to talk with
her pastor. She discussed the situation about Margo's pregnancy.

She also told her Sunday School Class. "I want to be the first to
tell you this, so you won't have to stop talking if I come up when
you are discussing it. You may criticize, or pray for us, just
whichever you please, but I feel that each of you will be praying
for us, for we certainly need your prayers."

The Pastor and the whole Church were very understanding,
and stood by to help in every way they could. Tacky felt God
had truly blessed them with wonderful friends.

Margo returned to school but had to stop again. Her high
temperature, chills, and blood passing through the catheter
started again.

One morning at two o'clock, Tacky had to take Margo to the
hospital. Her temperature was 106, and a lot of blood was passing
through her catheter. After a week in the Decatur hospital, a room
became available and she was transferred back to Spain
Rehabilitation.

Dr. Stokes asked the Infectious Disease Department, the
Obstetrics Department and the Urology Department to check Margo
and determine what was best for her and the baby. A special nurse
checked her every hour, because Margo wouldn't know when she
entered labor.

On Monday, December 27, 1971 Tacky returned to Birmingham
for company business and stopped by the hospital to see Margo.

"She's ready to go into labor soon," Dr. Stokes said. "The
baby isn't due until February, but, with all her kidney trouble,
we're expecting it at any time. Go back home and do your job. I'll
watch her closely. When she goes into labor, I'll send her to
University Hospital by ambulance and will call you."

Tacky was very tired when she arrived home. She took a hot
shower, dressed in her pajamas, packed a suitcase to be
prepared if a rush call came in, and talked to a friend on
the phone.

They'd been talking for only a few minutes when the operator interrupted them.

"Excuse me, I have an emergency call for Mrs. Lula Knox." They hung up and the operator connected the line for Dr. Stokes.

"Mrs. Knox, I have just sent Margo to the hospital by ambulance. I'm sorry to call you back down so soon, but she's dilating, and her contractions are very strong. Please hurry, but drive carefully."

Tacky called the friend back to tell her the news, and ask her to call her boss and Pastor. She called Rocky and told him the news and dressed as hurriedly as possible. Then, she got her suitcase, kissed Mama goodbye, and left.

When she arrived at University Hospital, she learned Margo was in the labor room, but Tacky could see her.

Margo was having hard chills. Her body shook, and her teeth and chin chattered. Tacky felt her forehead and knew her temperature was very high. Someone wheeled in an oxygen machine.

The doctor said, "This is for the baby's protection. Such high temperatures will cut off the baby's oxygen supply and might cause brain damage."

The doctors had planned to do a C-Section to deliver the baby, but her infection was so severe that it would mean instant death for Margo. Representatives from the three departments of Infectious Disease, Obstetrics, and Urology met every hour, wondering what to do. They never faced such a difficult case before.

They kept Margo packed with tylenol suppositories, but her temperature refused to drop. Soon, they packed her body in crushed ice. Tacky stood by, rubbing and massaging Margo's neck and jaws, trying to stop her teeth from chattering.

After two days and nights, one of the obstetric doctors said, "Mrs. Knox, I don't know how you stand this. There isn't a mother anywhere we would allow to be with her daughter in such a situation. You seem to know more to do for her than we do."

"I've already been through days and nights of this high temperature, chills, and shaking with her before we brought her in. I keep praying and doing what I can to comfort her."

He put his arm around her. "You really are one hellava lady!" Tacky smiled.

Dr. Stokes couldn't stay away from the Labor Room. He was so concerned about Margo's physical condition, and what her mental condition would be when the baby arrived. He gave Tacky his phone numbers every place he would be, and said to call the minute the baby came, day or night. He came by every day before and after work and on his lunch break.

On Thursday Morning, December 30, 1971 he walked in wearing his burgundy pants.

Tacky said, "Oh, Margo, look what Dr. Stokes has on. He means for you to do something today!"

Dr. Stokes blushed. "I swore I'd never wear these again, but I did it for you. I wanted to shock you into having that baby."

Margo smiled weakly. "I promise to deliver it today," she said faintly. Wait and see."

Dr. Stokes patted her on the shoulder and said, "I sure hope so."

In a few hours, Margo dilated even more, and the doctors were able to bring out a tiny baby girl. She was the most beautiful little girl Tacky ever saw. Her head was covered with wet, blonde ringlets, and she had a pug nose and perfect fingers and toes. Although she looked just fine, the nurses whisked her off to the high-risk clinic to check her for ailments.

Tacky rushed to the phone to call Dr. Stokes.

"Dr.Stokes, this is Margo's mother. She has just delivered the most beautiful baby girl you ever saw. Everything about her looks just fine. Those red pants of yours must have some special power." She laughed.

When Tacky returned to the room, Margo smiled. "Wasn't she beautiful?" She was so weak, but all smiles.

"The prettiest thing I ever saw since you were born. What will you call her?"

"Well, I don't know. I thought of Shane, thinking it would be a boy. My OB doctor has a son named Shawn, so maybe I could still call her Shane. What do you think?"

"Just spell it with a "y," and it will be fine."

"You mean like S-H-A-Y-N-E? I hadn't thought of that. It would be different, wouldn't it? I'll call her Terra Shayne."

"Sounds good to me. We should thank God for protecting her through all she's been through and helping her develop so well."

"I've been doing that ever since I saw her. She's so precious."

A doctor walked in, and said, "We must begin this unit of blood immediately, then you will be moved to another room where you can get some well deserved rest."

After several blood transfusions, and antibiotics, Margo's infection and high temperature were brought under control, and she was able to go home in a few days. However, she couldn't take Shayne with her. They wouldn't dismiss her until they had run all kinds of tests. The doctors were convinced that she had to have picked up some of the infection, or some abnormality was lurking some place in that little body. It just wasn't medically possible, they reminded Margo, for the baby to be normal after all she had gone through.

When Margo came home from the hospital, her paraplegic supplies were only twenty dollars a week less than Tacky's entire

income. Tacky wondered how she was supposed to work, make a
living, pay her bills, care for her paralyzed daughter, and tend a
newborn. She had her own health problems, too.

However, no job was too big for God, so Tacky cried out to Him
as she'd always done before.

A friend who played in Etheridge's band when they were in
college heard about Margo's accident and called one night.

"Mama Knox, I'm the purchasing agent for a Gadsden hospital.
If you get me a list of what Margo needs, I can get them for you
at hospital cost. That'll save you quite a bit of money."

"I can also autoclave Margo's irrigation fluid along with the
hospital's and save you that fee, too. All you'll pay is for the
medication."

That saved her sixty dollars per bottle. He spoke with his
suppliers, and they gave her medication samples, adding leg bags,
bed bags, irrigation syringes, and pads they could deduct from
their taxes. Being given all those supplies allowed Tacky to keep
her home.

After seven days of testing, the doctors said Margo should
take her baby home and treat it normally. Even though Terra was
premature, and it was medically impossible for her to be normal,
they couldn't find anything wrong with her.

Tacky and Margo thanked God for His goodness and protection
for Shayne. Tacky still had to take the baby to the hospital each
month for blood work and other tests, but only because the doctors
couldn't believe she was all right.

Terra Shayne had been through so many tests right after
birth, every time Tacky brought her back for more, she began to
hyperventilate and fret. Tacky comforted her and let her know it
wouldn't be the same, but she always came home with a temperature
for the rest of the day.

She grew so quickly it was unbelievable. When Tacky came home from work feeling tired and wondering how she'd manage all the work that faced her in the house, Terra's presence made her feel wonderful. She cooed, gurgled, and kicked her little feet.

After the first few nights, Terra slept all the way through the night, and Tacky learned to get up every hour to turn Margo without really waking up. She always woke on time, without setting her clock, and hardly knew she'd been up.

Before Tacky left for work in the morning, she helped Margo take her supplements for bowel movements, then bathe, dress, and help her into the wheelchair with a pillow across her lap with Terra on it. It was amazing how their lives fell into place. Instead of being a hardship, Terra was a blessing.

Margo rolled through the house with the baby on her pillow and thought of Jerry Clower's words, *Ain't God good?*

CHAPTER TWENTY ONE

Rocky was having trouble dealing with the situation and his relationship to it. It wasn't easy to consider tying himself down to a paraplegic the rest of his life.

When Tacky learned about the baby, she told him, "Rocky, unless you love Margo and the baby enough to treat them the way a wife and baby need to be treated, despite all the adversity, please don't consider marrying Margo. It will take a lot of love and patience to compensate for the added burden. If you marry only to give the baby a name, please don't do it. Two wrongs never make a right. I will do everything in my power to give them a happy home."

He couldn't seem to stay away, though his visits became more and more infrequent. Eventually, he began dating someone else. Margo felt torn, but she didn't blame Rocky. She realized she was in no condition to become a wife, though that didn't help her broken heart. Some nights, she cried herself to sleep. Giving up Rocky was more difficult than losing the ability to walk.

Mike bought land near Tacky and began building so he and Marie could marry. The house was finished just after Christmas.

Tacky

They purchased their furniture and were married in Marie's Baptist
church on January 21, 1972.

At the reception, Margo's three-week-old baby was passed
around and fussed over by all present. She was called the miracle
baby due to her circumstances.

Marie and Michael were a lovely bride and groom. Tacky was
grateful to have such a precious daughter added to the family.

Marie finished business college and got a job. Mike returned
to the old plant when he left the service. He worked a split
shift, and he didn't get to see Marie as often as he liked.

He wanted to go into business for himself and discussed it
with Tacky. The service station near their home was for
sale, so he bought it, then built a garage, and began repairing
cars.

As soon as Margo regained her strength, she returned to
cosmetology school. A neighbor with a six-month-old baby
agreed to keep Shayne during the day.

The pastor at their little country church asked Margo to join
the Youth Choir, because she was a good alto, which they needed.
She busied herself with school, work, and church. The church
accepted her and Shayne with love and kindness.

People began asking the Youth Choir to come to different
churches to sing. They arranged a singing tour to Florida and
back. Afterward, they often went swimming. Margo wanted to swim,
too, but no one thought it possible for her to stay afloat without
using her legs. Margo kept saying she could do it, so the older
boys helped her in and watched her carefully as she swam. She did
just fine.

Margo put everything into her studies. Many people said she
didn't have to study so hard, because her teachers would pass her
out of pity.

"I don't want favors," Margo said, because I'm in a wheelchair. I want what I can earn."

One day, Margo called Tacky at work. "Mother, can you come get me? I have diarrhea and ruined my clothes."

Tacky left work, placed towels from the trunk on the seat, and went to get Margo. At home, she spread a large towel on the bed and pulled off Margo's smelly clothes, then gave her a pan of warm soapy water for bathing while she took the dirty clothes outside to hose off before running through the washer.

Tacky used clean soda water to sponge Margo off and eliminate any odor. While she took that water out, she gave Margo some deodorant powder to sprinkle on.

Finally, she helped Margo dress. "I'm ready to return to school," Margo said.

"You don't have to go back today. You might have another accident."

"True enough," Margo remarked. "But I can't stay home just because I may have another accident."

"I might have an accident tomorrow or the next day, but what I can't help, I refuse to be embarrassed enough about to quit."

Back to school they went.

Tacky saved Margo's small social security and veteran's pay after Cran died. She bought her a car that had room behind the driver's seat for a folded wheelchair, then she took Margo to Birmingham to have hand controls mounted on it and get her paraplegic driver traiing.

Tacky and Margo didn't know that a permit was required before training could begin. Since they drove so far, the instructors agreed to let her drive the training car around the block while her own car was being altered, just to show her how to use the controls.

They explained the functions of the hand controls, then

Margo began driving. "Oh, you have already driven with hand controls before," the instructor exclaimed.

"No. This is my first time."

"You sure don't need any training. You handle it like a pro. You might as well get your permit and come back next week for your driver's test."

A few months after Margo began her cosmetology training at Calhoun Junior College, Mr. Roberts called the Decatur *Daily* and asked them to come over and take a picture of him with Margo. He was so proud of her, and the work she did. He confessed he'd been wrong to refuse her admittance.

When she completed her course, she drove herself to Montgomery, two hundred miles away, to appear before the State Cosmetology Board for her final exams. She received the highest cosmetology score ever given in the state of Alabama.

She heard that the owner of Fashionaire Beauty Salon had a new building with enough room for a wheelchair to maneuver, so she contacted the woman about a job. Workers were paid a percentage of what they brought in, so the owner was willing to give Margo a chance. She really didn't think it possible for someone in a wheelchair to make it, but she felt sorry for her.

Later, she said, "Hiring Margo was the wisest decision I ever made. Not only was she soon bringing in more than any other hairdresser, she had such a carefree attitude without complaints that the other workers were too ashamed to complain."

By the time Shayne was a year old, she seemed to know just the medications Margo took each morning and evening. She always wanted to get Mommy's medicine. Tacky had to read the labels to remember which ones were for mornings or evenings, but Shayne always got it right. She seemed to feel responsible for Margo and loved running errands for her.

Tacky

When Margo tucked her in at night, Shayne said, "Good night, Mommy. I wuv you. If you need me, just wake me."

When she was outside playing, she always talked to herself. If Margo couldn't hear her, she rolled to the door and called. Shayne always came running.

"Here I are, Mommy, what you want?"

"Mother just wanted to know if you were OK."

"I awwight, Mommy. Now can I go pay?"

Margo hugged her. "Just stay in the yard where Mommy can hear and see you."

"O-TAY!" She would say as she ran off to play.

When Margo wanted to tease Tacky, she called her Lu Lu.

One Saturday, Tacky was cleaning house and Shayne was in the bathtub playing. She got tired and called, "Nana, come get me out of dis bathtub."

Tacky wanted to finish vacuuming first. "Nana can't come right now. Wait just a little longer, and I'll be there."

"Nana, if you don't get me outta dis tub wite now, I'll call you LU LU!" she called.

Tacky smiled and went to the door. "You call me that, young lady, and you can stay in there."

Shayne giggled.

She was a bright, perceptive child, and always happy. She made every day enjoyable.

One afternoon when Tacky had to work late at the office, Margo and Shayne had already eaten when she finally came home. As she prepared a plate, Shayne said she wanted one, too.

"You have already eaten," Grandma told Shayne.

"I know. I want it for Lee."

That was the neighbor's German Shepherd that was always at their house.

Tacky

Tacky placed some food on a paper plate and Shayne took the plate to Lee. When she returned, she put the empty plate in the garbage.

"Did you feed all that food to Lee?" Grandma asked.

"No, Ma'am."

"What did you do with it?"

"He ate it all by himself."

Tacky almost choked on her food. Shayne thought she meant she had to feed the dog each bite!

Tacky, Margo, and Shayne rushed after work to get to a program at church when Grandma was visiting relatives out of town one day.

Margo called Tacky at work and said, "Mother, when you pick Shayne up at the Nursery School, why don't you go by Burger King and get some hamburgers and french fries? We won't have time to fix a meal tonight. By that time I'll be finished here and will meet you at home."

On the way home, Shayne said, "Nana, can I have some fwyes?"

Tacky spread a napkin in her lap and set two or three fries on it as she drove. Shayne folded hands and shut her eyes, and said. "Lord, I sank ooh for dese fwyes. Amen."

Tacky smiled. "That's a sweet girl. We must always be thankful for the blessing the Lord allows us to have."

Margo was just getting her wheelchair out of the car when they arrived home. After they went in, Tacky washed her hands, then got out paper plates and napkins and set burgers and fries on each plate. She cut Shayne's hamburger into small pieces for her.

As they sat around the table, Shayne said, "I want to sank de Lord."

"Lord, we sank you for dese burgers wit meat in dem."

Tacky

Margo looked at Tacky and grinned. "Mother, have you been serving my baby meatless burgers?" She laughed.

When Shayne rode in the grocery cart as Tacky bought groceries, she never ceased to amaze Tacky with her knowledge. Whatever was near, she asked, "Nana, do we need peanut butter or Rice Kwispies?"

It was as if she she could read. On the way home one day, they passed a Wal-Mart truck, and Shayne said, "Nana, dat was a big Wal-Mart truck."

"How did you know that?"

"It says Wal-Mart on the side."

"I know that, but how do you?"

They were never able to spell words around Shayne, either. One evening, Margo said, "Mother, why don't we ride out and get an i c e c r e a m." Shayne said, "I want some ice cweam, too!" They looked at one another in amazement.

In Wal-Mart one day, Margo said to Tacky, "I'd like to have some f r i t o s if I can find them."

Shayne said, "Mommy, here are the Fritos."

Tacky

Chapter Twenty-Two

On May 27, 1978, Marie gave birth to a slightly premature son they named Jeremy. She and Mike were ecstatic. Mike thought there was nothing like his new son, and he wanted to be at the hospital every feeding time to give him his bottle. That tiny little fellow wrapped his fingers around Daddy's heartstrings from the very beginning. He couldn't wait to get his wife and son home.

Two men wanted to rent Mike's garage for rebuilding cars. He added a new section for his repair work and leased it to them. Soon, the partnership dissolved, and one of them left. His only excuse was that he felt unhappy with the work.

Mike was good at repairing and selling, so he went into partnership with the remaining man. He soon realized his new partner wasn't always honest.

He told him, "I can't be partners with a dishonest man. I don't want to spend my nights worrying about dishonest deals made during the day. We'll dissolve the partnership, but I won't take the building back until your lease runs out."

Tacky

Mike bought more land a few miles up the road and built
another building. He and the first partner began rebuilding and
repairing damaged cars. After rebuilding one car, they soon got
several others in to work on.

They came to work Christmas Eve Morning to put a stripe down
the side of the car they had finished. When they unlocked the
door, gas fumes almost knocked them down. The propane gas line
had been disconnected from the heater, paint thinner had been
poured all over the outside of the new car and others in the shop,
and white paint poured on the red velvet interior of the car.

A panel had been removed from the back of the metal building.
Someone went in, did all that damage, replaced the panel, then dug
a trench several hundred yards away, and filled it with flammable
fluids. Then, set it on fire, slung the empty container out in the
woods, ran to his car and sped away.

A sudden hard rain came and put out the fire just inches from
the building. Mike called the police. Detectives and state
investigators searched the area and found a can that was used to
hold the flammable liquid thrown out in some thick bushes. Mike
recognized it as a special paint they used when he was in business
with the man who rented his other building.

Later in the day, when Mike and his partner were cleaning up
the mess, the previous partner walked in.

"My God, Doc, (his nickname for Mike), what happened here?"

Knowing he'd done the damage, Mike punched the man so hard he
split open his cheek. His partner had to pull Mike off the man
before he killed him.

He immediately went to town and swore out a warrent against
Mike for assault and battery. The sheriff, knowing the situation,
called Mike and told him to come in and sign his bond when he was
in town.

The first time it came up for trial, it was postponed.

Tacky

The ex-partner went to an insurance company and took out as much insurance as allowed on the contents of Mike's building he was renting, and continued his business. The day before the trial was to come up again, he moved his good equipment out, leaving a car he had fixed for a customer inside, and soaked the building down and set it ablaze in the middle of the night.

It burned so fast, it set the house next door, which Mike also owned, on fire, too. The fire department was able to save the house, but the garage was a total loss.

The trial was postponed again. When it finally came up several weeks later, the man's lawyer said, "Mr. Knox, they tell me you probably would've killed my client if your partner hadn't pulled you off him. Is that true?"

"It probably is."

"Have you ever thanked your partner for that?"

"No, Sir."

"Don't you think you should?"

"That remains to be seen."

In the courtroom, Tacky prayed, "Oh, Lord, please help Mike to be careful what he says."

Once all the evidence was presented, the judge said, "Mr. Knox admits to being guilty of assault and battery as charged. However, under the circumstances, there isn't a jury anywhere that would judge him guilty. I might've done even more than he did under the circumstances. I judge Mr. Knox not guilty."

Overcoming those setbacks wasn't easy, but Mike's honesty and hard work grew into a thriving business.

When Jeremy was little, he created an imaginary playmate for himself named Toby. Toby was his constant companion. He always wanted an extra plate set at the table for Toby.

Tacky

One night, Mike and Marie were going to Huntsville with some friends for dinner, and Colbert and Tacky kept Jeremy. He cried as they left.

"Don't cry, Jeremy," Tacky said. "Mother and Daddy won't be away long, and you can have a good time with Nana and Grandaddy."

"I know," he sniffed. "They let Toby go, but wouldn't let me go."

Tacky smiled, "No, they didn't let Toby go, either!"

"Uh huh, I saw him get in the car."

"While you were crying, they made Toby get out."

Looking out the window, he said, "Oh, there he is out on that highway! Toby, you get in here before you get hit by a BIG TWUCK!"

They didn't return by bedtime, so Colbert went to bed, Tacky dressed for bed and asked Jeremy if he would like to lie down until Mother and Daddy returned. He said yes but wanted the light left on.

Colbert's brow furrowed. "That's all right, Nana. Cut out the light. It hurts Toby's eyes."

He played with Toby until he began nursery school.

At the age of two, Jeremy went through a stage where everything was big. He saw a big truck, big dog, and big daddy. That went on until a neighbor took him to Sears one day, and he admired Winnie the Pooh. His oohs and aahs drew a crowd as he said, "Winnie de Poo got big eyes. Winnie de Poo got big ears. Winnie de Poo got big mouth. Winnie de Poo got big hands. Winnie de Poo got big feet."

People smiled and remarked how cute he was, then he turned and looked at them, saying "Winnie de Poo got big pecker!"

The neighbor immediately whisked him off through the laughing crowd. She later said she wanted to abandon him.

Tacky

Jeremy walked with Colbert and Tacky on church property behind
their house, talking as fast as he could. They passed the church's
tractor, and he said, "Nana, dat's a B I G TWACTOR! My BIG
Daddy drives a BIG TWACTOR sometimes, and a BIG CAR and a BIG
TWUCK." Tacky smiled and said, "Jeremy, You're so precious.
Nana loves you very much!"

"Uh Huh, I know, Jeremy love Nana too...BIG MUCH. Jeremy love
Daddy BIG MUCH TOO!"

After their walk, he played around his room awhile, then
went to the door and said, "Well, Nana, I gotta go."

"Where are you going, Jeremy?"

"I gotta go wuk. I can't make no money hangin' 'round here."
He grabbed the doorknob.

He started playing ball when he was in kindergarten, and
He was a big fan of the game. In 1986 he played baseball with the
Priceville Phillies. In '87, he was with the Priceville Yankees
in baseball, the Hartselle Minor Dolphins in football. Local
reporters liked writing about Jeremy's participation in winning
games.

After school was out, and Jeremy finished baseball and
basketball camps, Mike told him, "Son, you're going to have to
hurry and get through all your sports camps so you can help me at
the shop."

He grinned at his Daddy and said,

"Dad, I've just finished two camps. Next week, I'm going to
football camp. I'm thinking about taking tennis next."

Mike smiled. "I'll make you think of taking up anything other
than work, you little imp."

He was as full of mischief as his father. Tacky never knew
when one of them was telling the truth or fibbing. Mike had been
that way from the moment he learned to talk.

Tacky

In 1989, bad luck returned when Marie found a small lump on her breast. She saw a doctor, who performed a biopsy, and the results showed it was malignant. On December fourth, her thirty-ninth birthday, she had a radical mastectomy, removing the breast and twenty-one lymph nodes. The breast and fourteen of the lymph nodes turned out to be malignant. Doctors warned her the cancer might return.

She took the news well and decided to do what she could and leave the rest up to the Lord. She underwent chemotherapy for six months, along with over thirty radiation treatments and another operation. Still, she attended Jeremy's ball games, even when she was too sick to sit up or when her eyes wouldn't focus enough for her to tell who was at bat. It was important to be there for her son.

Mike and Jeremy kidded her like always. She laughed good-naturedly. They were her pride and joy. She came home from work each day and cooked good meals for them as if she weren't ill. Mike tried not to let his concern show, but the news struck him hard. They still had to go to Atlanta to ball games occasionally, and they went to Pennsylvania on vacation to see the races, which Jeremy enjoys so much.

Mike was so busy rebuilding cars, he didn't take much time off for pleasure, but he always saw his son play ball. Tacky was proud of that. She remembers how, after his own daddy's death, he asked after every game, "Mother, are you coming to my next ballgame?"

She, like Marie, tried to be at every one.

Tacky

CHAPTER TWENTY-THREE

Tacky's boss died suddenly with a heart attack, and the
insurance company sent people in to oversee the completion of the
the government contracts he began.

The company wanted Tacky to stay and finish the jobs, but
with her many expenses with Margo and the baby, she was afraid she
might be out of work soon, so she kept looking for other
possibilities.

One of the other women wanted to stay, finish, and draw
unemployment.

One day, the owner and plant manager of a local company
came in to purchase some of the equipment Tacky's company was
selling.

Tacky told them, "When anyone purchases this much of our
office equipment, they are required to take the Office Manager,
too."

They smiled and asked what her salary was. She didn't know
they were looking for a secretary. They called her coworkers to
ask how good she was. Finally, they decided it would be worth it
to pay more and hire someone who was qualified, so they offered
her a job. The other woman in the office would stay and finish off

181

the current jobs. She had a baby right around the time for final closing, so Tacky ended up returning to the office at the end of a regular workday and work late into the night to help the company finish.

Rocky came back into their lives to see Margo and Shayne. When Shayne was two-and-a-half, he added a room on the house he bought, made it wheelchair accessible, and married her on October 26, 1974. It was a simple, lovely ceremony at the little Baptist church Margo attended.

Tacky missed Margo and Shayne when they left, but she was glad to know they had their own home. She picked Shayne up after work each Friday afternoon and kept her until Sunday after church. That gave Rocky and Margo time alone, and was good for Tacky and Shayne, too.

Tacky began going out to eat with some of the workers, and she soon began dating a little. Cran had been dead more than twelve years by then, and she never had time for dating before, but, since the family was finally settled, she had more time for herself. Mike and Margo were both married, and Etheridge lived in Seattle following a musical career.

Mama visited her sister for several weeks at a time, because she felt Tacky didn't need her help as much. That gave Tacky additional freedom.

Tacky gave up all her night bookkeeping jobs except for her plant manager and his father, who ran a salvage business.

On March 3, 1976, Tacky went into the shop to deliver a message to one of the shop hands. As she returned, the phone rang. When she answered it, an excited voice said, "I can't find Mr. or Mrs. Lock, and the doors are all open. Would you please tell Wyman to come over and check this out?"

"I'm sorry, but he's out of town. I can send his brother, Derick, to see what's wrong."

She returned to the shop and told Derick the news.

"Daddy's at an auction sale," Derick said. "Mother's probably next door getting a Coke. As soon as I finish with these fluorescent lights, I'll go over."

Thinking she might save him a trip, Tacky called again, and a man answered the phone.

"Lady, please hang up and call the police. There's a lady hung in the back."

Tacky didn't want Derick to find his mother hung, so she ran back to the shop only to see him pulling out of the driveway. He didn't hear her shouting.

She rushed upstairs to the shop foreman. "Hurry down to the salvage store. Derick just left to go, and a man there said he found a woman hung in the back. I'm afraid it might be his mother."

Tacky hurried to her office and called the police.

A minute later, Derick called. "Tacky, the salvage store was robbed, and Mother's been killed. Will you please call Wyman and Harry?"

"I'm so sorry, Derick. Yes. I'll try to locate them."

She was looking up numbers of companies in Huntsville when she realized it was almost three o'clock. She decided to call Harry first. He'd be out of school any minute.

She called the school, but he'd already left. She didn't want to tell Wyman his mother was killed, so she called several businesses until she located him and said, "Wyman, I have bad news. The salvage store was robbed, and your mother was injured. Can you find your daddy and come in?"

"How bad is it?"

"It's very bad."

Tacky

"Tacky, please tell me the truth. Even if she's dead, it's easier to know now than wonder all the way home and find out when I get there."

"Wyman, I'm sorry to have to tell you this, but she's dead."

"Thank you, Tacky. I...I'll find Daddy and bring him in," he said in a shocked voice.

When Tacky got off work, she went by Wyman's home to see if she could be of any help. The family was devastated. She did what she could before going home.

Tacky never thought about entering a dark house alone before, but that night, it was shocking. She was glad when she finally stepped in, turned on the lights, and locked all outside doors.

Tacky was scheduled for bladder surgery on Monday, March 8th. She told Wyman she'd postpone it, because he needed her in the office.

He refused. He knew her gynecologist wanted her to have the surgery for some time, and she was having constant bladder infections. The doctor finally left her in an examining room while he called the hospital to set up her operation.

"You're scheduled for bladder surgery on March eighth at seven o'clock in the morning."

Tacky was shocked."You don't mean it! We need to discuss this further."

"I'm sorry, but it can't be put off any longer. You've gone too long already."

She tried to talk him out of it, but he refused to listen to her excuses.

With the recent tragedy, she didn't want to leave Wyman, but he was adamant.

"You're going ahead with the surgery," he vowed.

Tacky

     Wyman and Tacky were very close. He was plant manager, while she was office manager. They were able to discuss any problems with each other, business or personal, without inhibitions.

     The morning after her surgery, Wyman came to see her. He stooped over the bed to kiss her. "I guess I'll have to adopt you as my mother now."

     She wanted to say, "That'll be fine until Colbert finds someone," but she choked up too much to speak.

     Tacky, Wyman and his wife, Katherine, planned a picnic at Noccalula Falls and the Botanical Gardens when the azaleas were in bloom, but Tacky couldn't ride in a car at that time. The doctor would not let her ride for many weeks. In fact, the only way he would let her go back to work after six weeks was to have someone remove the heavy binder backs off her bookkeeping books, and promise not go up or down any stairs. She also had to lie down for half an hour in the morning, at noon, and in the afternoon. She wasn't allowed to lift anything heavier than her shoes for six months.

     Wyman and Derick watched her carefully to make sure she obeyed the doctor's orders. She appreciated their concern.

     In May, the doctor gave her permission to ride further, and Wyman asked if she still wanted to go on that picnic they had planned. Even though the azaleas were gone, there would be other pretty flowers, and the scenery was beautiful. They decided to go after Sunday School, since both were teachers. Wyman said he and Kat would pick her up after they left their church Sunday morning. Tacky promised to have a picnic lunch prepared.

     Early Sunday Morning, her phone rang.

     "Are you still up for our trip?" Wyman asked.

     "Oh, yes. I'm really looking forward to it. It's been a long time since I've had a real fun day.

"We feel the same way. . .by the way, would you mind if we asked Daddy to come along?"

"Of course not. It would be a wonderful trip for him. It might be just what he needs. I know how lonely he is."

When they drove up, Wyman and Colbert put the picnic supplies in the trunk.

Kat said "Pop,I'll get in back with Tacky,and you can ride up front with Wyman,"

"Just stay right where you are. Tacky and I will be fine back here," he replied.

They chatted happily, and Colbert patted Tacky's hand, saying, "You're some more, Girl."

Tacky smiled and thought of how loving and kind he was, so much like Wyman.

When they got to the falls, Colbert was attentive in helping Tacky over the rough spots as they wandered through the Botanical Gardens. It was such a beautiful spring day. The weather was perfect. They walked and chatted, and came back and spread the picnic lunch and everyone ate southern fried chicken, potato salad, macaroni and cheese, cole slaw and homemade rolls. They drank ice tea, and had little dried, fried apple pies for dessert.

"OH! How stuffed I feel," Wyman said. Everyone agreed it was time to try to walk off some of the stuffiness. They lingered at the water falls, enjoying the beautiful rainbow cast as the sun shone through the mist made from the spray of water from the falls. It was such a lovely ever-changing scene.

When the sun began to cast long shadows, they knew it was time to leave this lovely place, which had contributed so much to their relaxing and enjoyable day.

Wyman didn't want to end the lovely spell cast by the entire day, so he drove the long route home, back over Monsanta Mountain.

Tacky

It was so lovely to stop and look at the sunset from the high
mountain top; so peaceful after such a harrowing experience as all
had been through in the past few months.

They stopped in Huntsville and ate at a little cafeteria, and
then drove Tacky home. When they drove in the driveway, Lee, the
neighbor's big German Shepherd, ran all around the house then came
to the car door to walk Tacky to the house. Tacky patted him on
the head and told Colbert, who had gotten out to walk her to the
door.

"Lee is my protector. He always meets me at the car and walks
me to the door. I pat him on the head and tell him I love him and
appreciate him before going into the house."

Colbert said, "May I take Lee's place?"

Tacky laughed. It had been such an inspiring day. One she
would never forget. She thanked them and waved as she entered her
house. She thought of Colbert. He had that incredible gift of
friendship, full of wit and laughter. She liked his frank
openness on any subject.

The next day she and Wyman remarked about what a good time
everyone had. It seemed to have been just what was needed by all
of them.

About four o'clock, Colbert came into the office.

"How are you feeling after your long excursion yesterday?" he
asked.

"Just fine!" Tacky exclaimed. "How about yourself?"

"It was a wonderful day. So peaceful and joyful. I never
thought I could ever enjoy anything that much again," he
exclaimed.

"I'm glad you enjoyed it." Tacky smiled at him.

"I would like to ask a favor of you, if you don't mind." He
said to Tacky.

"What can I do for you?" She asked.

"I would like to come out and trim your shrubbery." He said.

Tacky thought, *He's feeling sorry for me now.* She never liked pity.

"Oh, that shrubbery will be OK until I'm able to trim it. I have electric clippers, and as soon as the doctor lets me handle something that heavy I can do it."

"Well, if I can't be of help to anyone, there isn't much joy in living is there?" He said in a dejected voice.

"Oh, if that's the way you feel. You can come and trim my shrubbery and I will cook dinner for you. How about that?"

"Sounds like a winner to me!" He exclaimed, as his eyes lighted up.

After the shrubbery was all neatly trimmed and dinner served and the kitchen cleaned up, they sat and talked until bedtime.

Colbert said, "I have some insurance papers I would like for you to look at and help me with when you have time."

"Sure. I'll be glad to, just let me know when." Tacky said.

"Do you have anything planned for tomorrow night?" He asked.

"No, that will be fine." Tacky said.

"Then, I'll pick you up about 6:00 and we will go out to eat. Is that OK with you?" he said.

After dinner, they came back and Tacky looked over the insurance papers and told him she would write a letter for him the next day that would take care of the transaction.

When he started to leave, he held out his arms, and Tacky gave him a little peck on the lips, and patted his arm.

He said, "Now what can I think up to get back out here tomorrow night?" Tacky laughed.

"Why not just say you would like to come back?"

"Will that get the job done?" He smiled at her.

"Why don't you try it and see?" she answered, smiling.

Later he told Tacky that was the coldest kiss he had
ever gotten. He had even had a warmer kiss than that from
his puppy.

Tacky laughed and replied, "It must not have been too bad,
you kept coming back!

"I thought I might be able to teach you how to kiss," he
laughed.

That first Saturday, they planned another picnic. This time
they would go to Warrior, Bankhead, and National Forest.
Tacky said, "I'll fix another picnic lunch."

"Oh no, there is no need to spoil the fun by working yourself
to death. I will bring some V8 Juice, a jar of peanut butter,
some crackers, and some Vienna sausage."

"Sounds fine to me." Tacky said.

Saturday morning, Tacky awoke to the sound of raindrops on
her roof. "Oh, there goes our picnic," she told Mama. While they
were eating breakfast. The phone rang. Tacky picked it up..

"Are you ready for that picnic?" Colbert asked.

"It's raining here," Tacky replied.

"Here, too. But I never let the rain spoil my plans."

"Well, I don't know what we'll do in the rain, but I'm game
if you are," Tacky retorted.

"I'll be right out!" he said.

"You're not going on a picnic on a day like this, I hope,"
Mama said.

"He says he never lets the rain spoil his plans, so I guess
we are." Tacky laughed.

"I've never heard of any such...and at your age."

Tacky laughed and kissed Mama on the cheek as she passed
by, and said, "At least it will be a new experience."

They enjoyed the leisure drive to the mountains, and when
they came to Brushy Lake, the rain had stopped. They got out and

walked the trails up around the bluffs and down to the water
falls, enjoying the walk and talk so much. Colbert confessed to
Tacky that he was having a terrible time dealing with forgiveness
for the murder of his wife.

"I know what the Bible says about forgiveness, but this was
all so uncalled for. Tina and I had forty-three years of married
happiness, and to have it all end so abruptly is hard to accept."

Later, they found that the sixteen-year-old boy they had
working for them, and who they were trying to rehabilitate, was
the one who committed the murder. He had gotten in an argument
with Tina over some equipment he wanted, cursed her out, and left.
He slipped back while she was watching T.V. and embroidering, cut
a skii rope and slipped up behind her, slung it over her head and
pulled it tight around her throat choking her. He got a vacuum
cleaner pipe and tied the rope around each end of it, pulled her
into the back room and raised it up to some shelves and hung her,
to make sure she wouldn't revive. He took the money she had on
her, and some articles in the store he wanted and left.

Colbert said, "I pray that God will help me to forgive him,
and I think I have about reached the point I can, then I awake in
the lonely hours of the night, missing her, and all my bitterness
and rage boil up in me again."

Tacky put her arms around Colbert and said, "I know it must
be terrible. I know the loneliness of the past fifteen years
without Cran. But a murder like that even makes it worse. We must
pray that God will give you the power to forgive him, for you will
never find peace until you do. There is no way you can do it on
your own, the strength will have to come from God."

"If he would just show some repentance. I think I could do
it, but I'm told that he brags about it to the others in jail."

They stopped under the bluff and held hands and prayed
that God would give Colbert the desire, the strength, and the

Tacky

power to forgive even though it was not asked for, nor even desired by the murderer. They walked on quietly to the falls, hand in hand, each thinking their own thoughts of heartaches, yet there were so many blessings as well. The falls at Brushy Lake were much smaller than at Noccalula, but were peaceful with their soft, murmuring sounds. They stood there for a long time hand in hand, and Colbert began making up a poem:

Today we saw trees, rocks, waters and land,
as we walked through the forest hand in hand.
We stood at a waterfall, with her hand in mine,
And gave God thanks for Peace of Mind.
This is not for the world to understand,
Just two lovers walking through the forest hand in hand.

Tacky's heart seemed to skip a beat as she felt a kindling of something that had lain dormant for so many years. In her mind, she cautioned herself to take it easy. This pain was new, and he really didn't know how he felt so soon after such a great loss.

They slowly walked back to the car and drove over to Old Pine Torch Church, one of the oldest churches in the state of Alabama. It is an old log church with drop windows with holes for rifles to shoot through. Tacky and Colbert sat on the old split log pews and held hands and asked God to guide their lives that they might live in obedience to His Will and Way. They talked of their lives with their first mates, and how hard the sudden loss was, but that life goes on, and each person must adjust to the sudden change as best they can.

They drove over to Natural Bridge and the rain stopped again. They spread their lunch and prayed that God would bless their food and lead them to know His Will for them.

It was one of the most beautiful picnics Tacky had ever enjoyed. It revived her love for the woods and flooded her

191

heart with memories of her childhood days when the woods held
so much serenity and were so precious to her.   She thought
of their whole day spent mostly in the woods, how peaceful and
enjoyable it was. They had rambled all day without the slightest
thought of anything contrary to her quaint Victorian upbringing.
Through the years of trouble and trials, she had not been
privileged to find the peace and refuge she had always found in
the woods. It was such a thrill to find someone that had a
sincere love for nature's wonderland. It gave him the same sense
of calmness and security it held for Tacky.

That night he wrote a poem about the singing of a little
bird, he called,

"Our Little Preacher Friend"
We listened to a little feathered preacher today.
As he stood in his pulpit high in a tree.
He preached without thanks or praise,
He preached to us about the love of God.
As the breeze moved the trees,
He seemed to say
'This is God's Message for today
In his words this little preacher summed up
Everything he had learned about life...
It goes on...despite our fears and wonders...
Life goes on!
He preached and sang, then flew away.
This was his message for today.
We walked on and felt the message
From this little preacher, clear...
The message God gave him, for us to hear.
When he stops again his message to bring,
I hope someone will listen to him,
And appreciate it as he sings!

Thank you, God, for the woodland so dear,

And help us always, Your Message to hear!"

"LOVE ONE ANOTHER"

The shadows were lengthening as the end of the day approached. There was very little talk on their way home. Each was reminiscing over things of the past and the enjoyment of this day.

Mama was standing at the door, as they drove up. Tacky looked at Colbert and said,

"I can just hear Mama saying, "How in the world could anyone enjoy a picnic on such a rainy day, and be gone the entire day!"

He laughed. "It was a wonderful day! It only rained showers when we needed to be driving."

"I was thinking of that, too. God is so good to us!"

"I know you are tired, and I need to get home to feed Tip; I'm sure Mama is wanting to know what happened today," he laughed.

"You're right! Mama isn't used to me being out like this!"

Colbert gave her a light kiss and said, "Have a good night. I'll see you tomorrow."

"Oh what a day!" Tacky exclaimed as she came in.

Mama was anxious to hear about their day in the rain. But when she saw Tacky she didn't have to ask. Her eyes were shining bright as the fireworks on the fourth of July. She was beaming like Mama hadn't seen in many years.

She said, "Tacky it must have been some day the way your eyes are shining."

Tacky laughed and hugged her. "Mama, do you remember how I loved the woods when I was a child?"

"Oh yes, you spent every leisure minute you could get in the woods as a child."

"Yes, and it has been so long since I had the opportunity that I had forgotten the extreme pleasure and awesomness God's Beautiful Nature Wonderland holds for me."

"Well I'm glad you enjoyed it."

That night when she went to her room she told herself,

"Tacky, don't lose your marbles...you must realize Colbert is not responsible for his feelings right now. He is so lost without Tina he is grabbing at straws, and you don't need to take him too serious." Nevertheless, her heart strings had certainly been plucked, and the tune was lovely to hear.

The weeks passed so swiftly. Colbert was at Tacky's door every evening when she arrived from work, or five minutes afterwards. They would ride over the mountain or along the river and just enjoy the lovely scenes of nature that God had planted everywhere. Tacky had been too busy earning a living to see these beauties for so many years. Now that she had to take it easy because of the bladder surgery, this turned out to be a special time for her. Colbert helped her with grocery buying, not letting her lift anything.

These afternoon rides, preparing meals together, and Saturday Picnics made Tacky feel like a young school girl again. Her heart rippled with joy and happiness. She couldn't understand the things that were happening to her. Any other time in her life, she would not have had time for the fellowship of a man. She always had a garden to work, the yard, canning and freezing, the house to clean, besides cooking and sewing for a family. But since this surgery, the doctor would not let her do any hard work. She thought of how lonely and depressed she might have been had Colbert not come into her life just at this time. He and his sons watched her like a hawk. If she ever started to pick up anything a little heavy, or go up and down steps, they immediately stopped her. What would she have done without them?

Tacky

After Colbert left one night, Tacky began thinking seriously.
She was at the fork of a road. The children were all on their
own, Mama spent much time with her sister in Centre and her son in
California and Collinsville, and her grandchildren in Arizona.
Her home was with Tacky, but she was also enjoying her own freedom
now. Tacky's time was pretty much her own for the first time. The
times with Colbert became more precious each time they were
together. They had prayed time and time again for God to let them
know if they were right for one another. Tacky had been a widow
for more than fifteen years, had more surgeries than she had
fingers and toes, all over her body, plus a complete hysterectomy
and a bilateral mastectomy. *Could I ever make a man happy?*
Especially one, who was accustomed to a wife that had never had
any surgeries, one who had all her female organs and lovely
breasts, was a beautiful and talented lady. Could Colbert ever
adjust to me as I am? Are we right for each other? I know I
could never fill Tina's shoes. Could I adjust to having someone
boss me again after all these years? We always feel at peace
when we pray about it, but is that because this is what we want,
and not God's Will after all?'
Tacky dressed for bed, read her Bible and fell on her knees
beside her bed, she had to know one way or another, for she had to
stop seeing Colbert if this was not the right choice for them.
She prayed her heart out to God.

"Lord, every time we are together becomes more precious than
the time before. We are both going to be terribly hurt if it is
not in Your Will for us to marry. We are in no hurry, but I must
know your Will. I don't want to be hurt and I don't want to
hurt Colbert. In Your Word, You gave Gideon an answer to his
prayer, that he couldn't question. I am putting out my fleece as
Gideon did, please let me know, no later than in the morning
whether this is within Your Will. You are the only one that

knows if we could be happy together, and if we could serve You better together or separate. Please give me some sign I can't question. Thank You for hearing my prayer. Amen."

She crawled in bed, cut out the light, pulled the covers up over her and snuggled down to go to sleep, leaving everything in God's hand.

Tacky's thoughts were filled with an intense desire to serve the Lord to the best of her ability. It seemed as if God entered her room and said: ."Get up, get your Bible and read Psalms 37:4 and 5." She jumped up, turned on the light and grabbed her Bible. She had no earthly idea what Psalms 37:4 & 5 had to say to her, but she read; "Delight thyself also in the Lord; and He shall give thee the desires of thine heart. Commit thy way unto the Lord; trust also in Him; and He shall bring it to pass." Tacky was so excited. She said, "Lord, Thank You, I do delight in You and in Your Word, and I try to commit my way unto You, and I do trust You to bring it to pass, and I will not doubt again that it is within Your Will."

Tacky knew that to keep the heart open meant running the risk of being hurt, but now she was willing to take that risk. She called Colbert and told him about her prayer.

He said, "I never doubted in the first place!"

"But Colbert, I had to be sure! I didn't know if I could make you happy, and I sure didn't want to cause you more pain."

"I sure never doubted that! I do appreciate you seeking the Lord's Will in it, though. You are some woman! And I Love you!"

Tacky kept praying for Colbert that he would be able to forgive the terrible crime committed against his family.

One day after many sleepless nights, he was driving down the highway, still struggling with his burden of forgiveness. God's Holy Spirit seemed to speak to him with this thought,

'At most, he only took a few short years away from your wife. He destroyed her body, but not her soul. He only caused a premature entrance into heaven. Any punishment he receives, you must leave to the law."

He told Tacky, "I want to see the murderer's soul saved. Through the interceding of the Holy Spirit, a feeling of pity has replaced my feelings of hatred and desire for revenge. I'm now able to forgive and receive God's peace. I could find no peace and harmony in my life as long as I harbored malice and revenge in my heart. Jesus gave me comfort through the words of John, Chapter 14:26, 27a:"

"But the Comforter, which is the Holy Ghost, whom the Father will send in My name, He shall teach you all things, and bring all things to your remembrance, whatsoever I have said unto you. Peace I leave with you, My peace I give unto you."

"Tacky, I have that peace in my life once again. I am so thankful Jesus knows all my needs and will supply them at the time I need them so badly. You have helped me so much by your continual praying. I know we are going to have a wonderful life together!"

"Thank the Good Lord, our prayers have been answered. I am so thankful that you have been able to forgive, and find the peace that only forgiveness can bring. If we didn't have the Holy Spirit, and Christ's forgiveness, we'd never be able to have any true peace and joy in our lives."

"That's true, and together and with God's leadership, I foresee a great togetherness for us," Colbert said as he took Tacky in his arms and held her close.

Tacky

CHAPTER TWENTY-FOUR

While waiting for the trial to sentence Tina's murderer,
there were so many strange things happened to Colbert.
Someone cut up a black cat and placed it almost dead in his
shrubbery. It was crying for help as it couldn't move. He
found it and had to kill it. A few days later another black
cat was found dead with flies around it. Sometimes he would
come in at night and everyone would have lights but him. He
was on a separate transformer, and someone shot the fuse
several times leaving his house in darkness. One Saturday he
came in and a special piece of shrubbery out near the
driveway had been twisted off near the ground and a bottle of
beer and a whiskey bottle filled with blood was lying there.
His son, Hal, who lived next door was called one morning
around 1:00 a.m. When he answered the phone someone talking
in a muffled voice, said, "You had better check on your
Daddy, something bad has happened to him." He called him
immediately, and Colbert told him he was o.k. it was just
someone probably playing a prank. This was just after there
was so much in the news about the Manson Murder Trial, in
California. Someone was copying some of the things that had

been done in that situation.

Finally the trial came up for the young man that had done the killing, and he was convicted of first degree murder, and sentenced to fifty years in the pen. All the strange happenings ceased after this.

After things settled down Tacky and Colbert were married in a simple but beautiful little wedding ceremony by her pastor, at the little Baptist Church she attended. Tacky wanted to use their grandchildren as attendants for their wedding.

Wyman's two Stepsons were Ushers, ages sixteen and seventeen.

Derick's two sons were Best Man and Ring Bearer, ages ten and seven.

His two Stepdaughters were Bride's Maids, ages ten and seven.

Hal's daughters were Maid of Honor and Flower Girl, ages nine and six.

Margo's daughter was also a Flower Girl, age four.

Etheridge flew in from Seattle, Wash. to sing.

Mike gave Tacky away.

Margo saw that the wedding guests were registered.

The daughters-in-law served at the reception.

They were married on a Saturday afternoon in October. After the reception they drove up to Wheeler Lodge to spend a couple of nights before leaving for Hawaii. The sun was sinking low as they drove, and it was the biggest Sun Tacky had ever been able to look directly at. It was so huge and red. It looked as if one could just reach out and touch it.

Tacky remarked to Colbert, "Isn't God Wonderful to Bless us with such a beautiful sunset. I don't think I have ever in all of my life seen a more beautiful one. I have never seen the sun look so close and yet you can look at it without it hurting your eyes."

"It is certainly unusual, to say the least!" Colbert
replied.

Colbert was such a thoughtful husband. Mama said, "It
will be wonderful, if it'll just last!" She just couldn't
believe a man could be so helpful and thoughtful around the
house.

They came back home Monday afternoon, washed up all
their clothes and packed them to go to Hawaii. Mama had a
ticket to California to go stay with her son, while they were
on their Honeymoon.

They took the eight island flight, and on the Island of
Kaukai, they rode down the Hanalia River, enjoying the
beautiful scenes as the entertainers from the Smith Boat
Lines sang love songs to them; when they took them to the
Fern Grotto they remarried them Hawaiian style. They looked
at their watches and it was one week to the hour and minute
of their wedding back home. It was so beautiful and
romantic. Tacky had never seen foliage as beautiful as grew
along the path to the fern grotto. It just looked as though
it had been oiled with baby oil. "No wonder this is called
the Garden Island," she told Colbert.

They saw the Island where the leper colony was formed
by Father Damion. They went to the Punch Bowl Cemetery, and
saw Ernie Pyle's grave, saw the Eternal Flame, and Pearl
Harbor. Tacky couldn't hold back the tears as she saw the
USS Utah and Arizona and the many memorials to the boys that
lost their lives in the Pearl Harbor Surprise Battle. She
thought of the loved ones back home that were so pained by
their loss.

When they came back to California and went to Church
with her Brother and family, the church bulletin had a
picture of a church with a couple walking with their arms

Tacky

around each other and it said, "TWO SHALL BECOME ONE!"
It seemed that everywhere they went and everything they did,
they just received extraordinary blessings! They didn't
realize life could be filled with so much joy after such
tremendous heartaches!

Tacky

CHAPTER TWENTY-FIVE

When Margo graduated with honors from cosmetoloy, and
was hired by Wanda Barnes at Fashionaire Beauty Salon, her
first customers sat on a stool or cushion in the floor
between Margo's legs for her to do their hair. She did lots
of manicures then, because she was not strong enough to
handle hair cuts and curls all day, but gradually they began
to experiment with her customers by lowering the beauty chair
as low as it would go and the customer turning in it where
she could get to them. Her friends encouraged her to get a
motorized wheelchair to make it easier for her, but she
declined.   "I need to build these muscles and letting a
motor do part of my work is not going to increase my
strength," she reasoned.

As her arms and body gained strength she soon was
handling her job efficiently and brought in as much money for
Wanda in three days as most of her other operators did in five.
She enjoyed her work and never lost her sense of humor. One
customer made a remark one day..."Margo, do you ever feel
bad? I have been coming to you for several years, and I have
never seen you when you acted as though you felt bad!"

Margo replied, "Complaining about our feelings does not make us feel any better. Therefore why complain?"

Rocky and Margo bought three acres of mountain property and Margo designed a log house to fit her needs. They had this house built, but they were to do the finish work. Margo stained logs from the floor to two of the top, which she couldn't reach. She stained doors and trim around the doors and windows. They were so proud when they were able to move into their large log house. All the rooms were extra large to give her room to get around in them in the wheelchair. Her outside doors were four feet wide, her hallway was five feet wide. She had a shower bath in her bathroom where she could roll in and bathe.

In her kitchen she could roll underneath the surface unit stove eyes to do her cooking and could roll under the sink. The house was built on a hillside with beautiful trees surrounding it. They could sit on the front porch and enjoy the lovely countryside.

When Shayne was ten she was home cooking one day. She asked her mom as she was going to work if she could make some doughnuts. She told her it would be all right, "Just be careful." She cautioned.

Shortly after Margo left for work Tacky got a phone call. "Nana, come quick, the house is on fire!"

"Shayne you just get out, and stay away from it. We'll be there as quick as we can make it." She said.

She called the fire department but Shayne had already called them. Colbert and Tacky grabbed fire extinguishers and took off, but when they got there it was going too strong for them to get into it. Shayne had burned her hand badly trying to get it put out.

Tacky and Colbert had someone to hook to the boat and

camper and pull it from under the carport, and they began
grabbing lumber and material that were stacked underneath the
carport and taking it away from the house. There was so much
smoke inside no one could get any furniture or anything out
of the house.

Someone called Margo and she came home. It was so sad
to watch their lovely home go up in smoke. Fire trucks from
Decatur, Priceville and Hartselle responded, but they
couldn't stop it before everything was ruined. They did keep
it from burning down, but everything inside was ruined.
Margo took Shayne to the doctor with her hand, it was so
painful. He said she had second and third degree burns on
it.

Shayne was very grieved at what she had done. She kept
crying, "I have burned our house down. Nana, My last
doughnut splattered grease out when I dropped it in and the
grease caught fire. I ran to the camper got the fire
extinguisher and put out the grease fire, but the window
curtain had caught. I tried to put it out but it had caught
the wood around the window on fire, and the extinguisher
didn't have enough fluid to put it out."

Tacky tried to console her. "Honey, you did everything,
even an adult could have done to put it out. Don't blame
yourself. God doesn't hold us responsible for things we
can't help. Throughout life we will do things that will
hurt ourselves or someone else, but if it is an accident and
something we couldn't help, God doesn't hold us responsible
for it. Just thank God that you were not burned any worse,
and pray that He will bring some good from it."

"How in the world could God bring any good from my
burning our house down?" She cried.

"I don't know, Shayne, but He tells us in Romans 8:28

that, "We know also that all things work together for good to those who love God, to them who are the called according to His purpose."

"This doesn't mean that just because we love God and try to serve Him, that everything that happens to us will be good. It means He can bring something good from our faults and failures, and trials, if we trust them to Him. and use them as stepping stones in place of stumbling blocks."

"I don't know how He can bring any good from this, but I sure am going to trust it to Him." She answered innocently.

Rocky, Margo and Shayne had to move in with Colbert and Tacky until they could get a trailer set up with a ramp, and the doors widened for the wheelchair. It had been several years since Margo had used a bathtub for bathing, and her legs fought the strain put on them. In the bathtub they would spasm kicking the sides of the tub as she got in and out until her heels or ankles would bleed. Shayne would cry and say, "It's all my fault." She was so upset over the extra hardships it caused her Mother. They had the same problem in the trailer, but at least they had a home again. They had replacement insurance, so it covered the cost of setting up the temporary trailer for them to live in.

They rebuilt the house. They realized had Margo been in the house when it caught fire, she would have had to roll through it to get out. So they added a door and a ramp at their bedroom, and made a few little changes to make it more convenient for her.

They did not refurnish it as elaborately as they had before. Rocky had all kinds of CB Equipment, and Margo and Shayne had musical equipment, piano, guitar, accordion, and so forth, which they did not replace. By being very careful in their choice of furniture, they were able to pay off the balance of the loan and had a new house and new furniture debt free.

Tacky told Shayne, "See how the Lord has blessed your family. Something good did come from it."

"Yes, Nana, and I am so thankful, but I sure wouldn't put Mother through all she went through for the debt-free home."

"Of course not, none of us would, but it is wonderful to have a nice new home and no more payments."

Rocky and Margo bought a cabin on Elk River, remodeled it. They bought a big pontoon boat and enjoyed the river, but it was so muddy after stormy weather, they sold their cabin and bought three acres of property on Smith's Lake. They bought a camper and camped down there most every week-end in the summer months. They dug out on the side of the hill near the lake and built a large boathouse with a boat ramp and a generated pully to pull it into the boathouse.

Later they built an A-frame house over the boathouse. They pumped water from the lake for the bathroom with a Generator-powered pump until they got electricity and water in that area. They hauled in their drinking and cooking water.

They throw Margo off the pontoon boat and she swims all around in the lake. She has never let her paraplegic condition be a complete handicap to her. She does anything anyone else does, except walk.

Rocky had foot pedals welded on his motorcycle and they would fasten her feet to the pedals and tie her on behind him and they would go motorcycle riding. They have a four wheeler down at the cabin, Rocky helps her on it and she rides all around visiting the neighbors and enjoying the mountains. They have big fish fries and invite all the neighbors in, and she does all the cooking and preparing for it.

She does all of her grocery buying, pushing the grocery
cart with one hand and rolls the wheelchair with the other.
She has lots of trouble with kidney stones. When they are
cutting into the bladder so badly her legs have a fit. Many
times at work they have taken electrical cords and wrapped
around her legs and wheelchair to keep the spasms from throwing
her from the wheelchair.

One day she had so much trouble all day with her legs
that when she came home from work she took her catheter out
and seven kidney stones from the size of the little fingernail to
the size of the thumbnail popped out. She had promised to
take some of the neighbor children to the fair that night at
midnight, as it was half price then, and that was the last day
and night it was to be in Decatur. The children didn't have
the money to go at regular price, so she stayed in bed until
about 11:00 p.m. then got up rolled into her shower, bathed,
rolled back to the bed, inserted a catheter, dressed and got
up and took Shayne and the children to the fair.

Tacky and Colbert were going on vacation and Margo was
having kidney problems but would not let them know. After
they left, she got in her car and drove to Birmingham,
checked herself into the hospital. The doctor thought they
could burst the stone with laser without putting her to sleep
so she wouldn't let anyone go with her. She was just going
as an outpatient and would be back home that night. But when
they applied the laser her legs spasmed so badly they broke
the straps they had strapped her to the table with and they
had to admit her to the hospital and put her to sleep and do
surgery to break up the stones and remove them. They had become
as large as a golf balls.

Three days later she was dismissed to go home. She was

taking muscle relaxers to keep her feet and legs from
spasming so badly, and got so sleepy several times on the way
home that she would run off the edge of the highway before it
woke her up. She was so thankful to get home, get her
wheelchair out and roll inside. She was looking forward to
getting in bed where she could relax and sleep. Just as she
rolled through the kitchen the phone began ringing. She
picked it up. "Oh, I'm so glad you're home. Shayne has been
badly hurt at school and needs to go to the hospital," The
school secretary said.

Margo rolled back to the car, got herself into it pulled
her wheelchair in and took off to school. Someone brought
Shayne and put her in the car. Her knee had been badly cut
and needed suturing. When she got to the hospital, she got
her wheelchair out, got into it, rolled around and had Shayne
slide into her lap and went rolling into the emergency room.
Afterwards she and Shayne were so glad to get home where
they could crawl in bed and rest.

Many times over the past thirty-seven years she has faced
great obstacles, but has always worked them out. She has a happy
home. She and Rocky love antiques and collect daisy churns,
irons and just about any old country antique they can come
across. One of the things she lost during the fire that
meant the most to her was a very old antique buffet her
mother had purchased at the Salvation Army Thrift Store when
they rented their first shack after Cran came home from the
army. They wanted to wait until they got their house built
before they bought nice furniture. They could never part
with this piece of furniture, though.

When Margo married, she had taken the buffet, stripped
it down to the natural wood and finished it, and it was a
prize possession with her. She has never been able to find

another like it. It took her month after month to get all
the finish stripped off, but she did it in her spare time,
without any help, she wanted to do it all herself. Several
people tried to buy it from her when they saw it as she was
working on it, but this had always been a piece of beauty to
her, and she could visualize the real beauty that lay
underneath the old finish, and wouldn't talk of parting with
it.

Their log house being on the steep hillside, kept Rocky
upset because he was constantly breaking lawn mower belts.
Also there was only one side of the yard that Margo could
roll in. And being out in the woods as it was and made of logs,
made their insurance so high, that they began looking for some
property on level ground.

Finally they purchased six acres in a new subdivision
about two miles from their log house. They sold their lovely
home and began building a new brick home. It has a porch on
two sides, and a carport on the back that eight cars could be
parked underneath.

Margo still passes lots of kidney stones, and calcium.

Shayne has been an unusual child. Her thoughts and
desires have always been worked out with consideration for
her parents.   On a survey at school, the question was asked,
"What are some of the things you cannot talk with your
parents about?"

Shayne was telling Tacky about it, and said, "Nana, I
don't know of anything in the world I couldn't talk with
Mother about!"

Tacky said, "Shayne that is wonderful! That's the way
it should be with every mother and daughter, but so many
children and parents don't have that close relationship. You
are one lucky little girl! Always try to keep the line of

Tacky

communication open with both parents, for it builds your
relationship with them and theirs with you!"
     The Miracle Baby has grown up, fallen in love and they
built a two-story house close to Margo and Rocky. When the
house was finished, they got married in front of the bay window in
her parents' home. She didn't want a church wedding, for she
didn't want her parents to be out all that expense, and she
wanted to put all she had saved on the house to lower the
loan amount. She has always been a very conservative and
mature person, saving her pay days so when she needed to trade
cars or buy anything major she would have the money and not have
to pay interest.

Tacky

CHAPTER TWENTY-SIX

Wyman purchased a bicycle built for two for Colbert and
Tacky shortly after they were married, because Tacky couldn't
ride a bicycle alone. Her crippled foot would not bend in
the ankle and she could not keep the foot pedals going all
the way over, but with Colbert pulling when they got to the
spot she could no longer pull with that crippled foot, they
could ride.

They had so much fun with the bicycle. Each morning in
the spring and summer they would arise before sun up and go
riding. Everything was so beautiful and peaceful at this
time of day. The early morning patches of fog here and
there, the birds hopping along in front of them or flying by
chirping contentedly, inspired Tacky to write:

BEGINNING A NEW DAY
Riding our bicycle built-for-two,
Early in the morning, through the grass wet with dew,
Thanking God for such a thrill,
As with His many beauties, our hearts are filled.
We look at the lovely green trees,
Listen to the rustling of their leaves,

Tacky

              As we enjoy the cool morning breeze.
         Such a joy to hear the cherry songs of the birds,
     And sympathize with the "late sleeper", by whom these
                   Inspiring sounds are never heard.
         What a spectacle as the sun comes creeping up...
                 So bright and beautiful, and so abrupt!
                   The patches of fog here and there...
                   Giving optical illusions everywhere,
                 Making the world a glorious fantasy land,
                   With so much beauty on every hand!
                   We thank God as together we ride,
                   Asking Him, our lives to guide.
             This is the beautiful beginning of our day,
             Which makes life so wonderful along our way!
         Many people smiled as they passed Colbert and Tacky
riding the tandem bicycle. It was quite unusual to see an
old man and woman riding a bicycle together.

         Rocky's sister drove the school bus, and she told Margo
one night when they were visiting, "Oh Margo, you wouldn't believe
what I saw this morning down at Priceville,when I started out to
pick up the children just at daylight...An old man and woman
riding a bicycle built-for-two! And they looked as though they
were having the time of their life!"

         Margo laughed, "That was my mother and step-dad! And they
were having the time of their life!"

         "Oh, it was so early I couldn't see who it was! But they
certainly seemed to be enjoying the ride together!"

         "Colbert has been such a blessing to Mother. I thank God
they are so happy. They both deserve happiness after all they
have gone through! It seems that they have a ball at everything
they do, whether it is riding the bicycle, working the garden,

canning, freezing, visiting the sick, or whatever they do, they do it together!"

Colbert told Tacky before they married, "When we marry, we want every day to be a new experience, for life can become dull if it becomes a set pattern where every day a certain routine is followed." He wanted Tacky to quit work so he could show her the beauties he and Tina had enjoyed in different places of the U.S.

"If we wait until you are old enough to retire, then we may not be able to travel and I might never be able to show you the beauties out there that you haven't seen."

Tacky worked about six months training another girl to take her job, then she only worked when someone was out sick or on vacation. They went out west and down to Florida. They went on a Carribean Cruise, and enjoyed places Tacky never thought she would ever have a chance to see.

Tacky

CHAPTER TWENTY-SEVEN

In September of 1980, Colbert had eye surgery. The doctor
removed a cataract and did an implant. He kept coming back to the
hospital all day to check the eye. Tacky thought that was
unusual. At 7:00 p.m. he came back and checked it again and said,
     "I'm sorry to tell you this, but we will have to go back and
take the implant out, his eye is rejecting it."
     Tacky called Wyman and asked him to get in touch with the
other family members, as they had gone out of town for the
surgery. He and his wife came over to Athens for the second
surgery.
     The doctor removed the implant and put a lense over the
eye. The next day he let Colbert go home, with a caution that
Tacky keep a close check to see that no infection set up.
     That night Colbert woke up in terrible pain. He had been
subject to kidney stone attacks for years, and recognized this as
another attack. Tacky called his doctor and took him to a local
hospital. They made x-rays and found two stones in the tube from
the kidney to the bladder. One was riding piggy-back on the other
and they could not pass. They prepared him for what they called

214

the basket surgery. They told Tacky they would be prepared to do further surgery to remove it if that didn't work.

After a few hours in the operating room the doctor came out and said he couldn't retrieve it without surgery. But he had not done the surgery. Tacky was pretty upset that they didn't go ahead and finish it all while he was put to sleep. They didn't tell her at this time, but they couldn't proceed further because his heart acted up. However, the next day they did put him to sleep again and operated to remove the stones. They located another in his kidney, but would have had to cut both from the front and back to remove all three, so they removed the two that were causing all the pain and left the other. After he came through the surgery without any further complications they told her why they couldn't finish it the first day.

Every day his eye doctor called to see how his eye was doing. Tacky told him it was looking great, and she was keeping it doctored just as he had told her. On the third day, he called and asked if she minded him coming over and checking it himself. "I don't doubt your word, but I would feel better if I could check it myself, since he's had this kidney stone surgery." He said.

"That's fine. I think it looks great, but I would appreciate your checking it too, if you have the time." She said.

He drove over to their town and came by the hospital and looked at his eye, and confirmed that it looked great. He was very pleased with it.

Tacky was having lots of trouble with a ruptured disk in the cervical area again. She was experiencing terrible headaches, and was about to lose the use of her right arm.

The third of January 1982 she entered the hospital in Huntsville for tests, which ended up in ruptured disk surgery

again. She had two cervical disks removed in 1966 and they
removed two more this time, and took bone from her hip to
fuse the spine together. She was doing fine a few days after
the surgery, and walked next door to talk with a patient who had
also had ruptured disk surgery. All at once it felt like
something hit her in the low back and she had terrible pains run
down both legs. She had a hard time making it back the few steps
to her room and bed. When her doctor came in she told him about
it. He pulled the sheet that was tucked under the mattress at the
foot of the bed and lifted her leg. When he raised it about four
inches from the bed she screamed with pain. When he lowered it
back to the bed the pain subsided.

"Please don't tell me I have a ruptured disk in my low back,"
she pleaded. "You did check the whole spine when you did the
mileogram test, didn't you?" She asked.

"Yes, it all looked fine except the cervical area. I think
you just have some pinched nerves that need some therapy," he
consoled her.

He ordered hip traction, heat applications three times a
day and whirlpool twice a day. She had to stay in the hospital
quite a bit longer because of the low back problem.

The last of January she was finally able to go home, but
was not able to be out of bed, she had to use the traction at
home.

The next morning after she came home, Colbert said,
"Something has happened to my eye. It looks as if a window shade
has been pulled down over half of it."

"Go call your eye doctor and tell him." Tacky said.

"Oh, it'll probably clear up after a while. I don't want to
worry him."

Tacky had a phone beside her bed, so she looked up his
number and called. His nurse said he was in surgery, but she

would call the hospital and tell him, and he would call as
soon as he finished the surgery.

In a few minutes the phone rang, and it was the nurse.

"Dr. Gates said, come to his office as quick as possible, and
he would see you between surgeries."

"This is probably a trip for nothing," Colbert complained as
he got his coat and cap to leave.

"I hope it is, but I'm afraid it isn't!" Tacky said.

Dr. Gates' nurse called as soon as he saw Colbert and said
they had been trying to locate Wyman to carry him to Birmingham to
the eye foundation. He had a detached retina, and needed
emergency surgery. They hadn't been able to locate Wyman, so
Tacky must have someone lined up to drive him down there as soon
as he returned home.

Tacky immediately called their Church Prayer Chain. Their
Pastor was in a meeting, which would be over in about fifteen
minutes, if they hadn't located Wyman by that time he would come
and drive him to the eye foundation.

When Colt came in, he said, "I'm not leaving until we locate
someone to come stay with you."

A friend that Tacky had met when she first moved to
Priceville called, and she told her about Colt's problem and
she said she would come and stay with her while he was in the
hospital.

Tacky said, "Jan, you couldn't have called at a better
time. I wouldn't have thought of you."

"It's just the Lord looking out for you." She said.

Their Pastor drove Colbert to Birmingham. Wyman got word
they were looking for him, shortly after they left, he and
his wife got ready and went on down to be there for surgery.

Tacky was very upset that she was unable to go with him.
Always before she had been able to take care of him when he

needed her, and it was so hard to have him go off without
her.

A week later, some friends went down after work to see
him, and about 10:00 p.m. that night they came in bringing
him home. The doctor had come in while they were there.
Colbert introduced them to his doctor and told him they were close
friends of his from home.

"Colt, I intended to keep you a day or two longer, but if
your friends have room to take you home, you are doing fine, and I
know you are lying here worrying about your sick wife at home so
if they don't mind, I'm going to let them take you home."

They were so glad to be together again. This was the
first time they had really been separated since their marriage.

The next day Tacky was sick at her stomach all day. She
was able to get up and down a little now, and sat up some. By
their regular bedtime she was very nauseated and lost all she had
eaten that day. She was very restless in bed but finally dozed
off to a fitful sleep. She awoke at 12:45 a.m. feeling as though
she had a band around her chest. She couldn't swallow and felt
like she was choking. She slipped out of bed without turning on
the light, for she didn't want to disturb Colt. She went to the
bathroom to get a drink of water to see if it would do away with
the choking feeling. She couldn't swallow it. She shut the door
and turned on the light. It was shocking as she squinted at the
reflection she saw in the mirror. Her lips were turned wrong side
out, and her jaws looked like she had baseballs in them. Her neck
and what she could see of her chest had whelps as big and thick as
her hand that were a Christmas red. She pulled up her pajama
top and her body was the same way. She looked at her feet
and legs: they were so swollen and red. Even the palms of her
hands were covered with white spots all through them.

She went back to their bedroom and turned on the light.

Colt opened his eyes, and she said, "Honey, look at me. What do you think is wrong?" He took one good look and said, "Good Lord, you are poisoned on something! Call Mike and get to the hospital as quick as possible."

When Mike got there, he said, "Goodness, Mother you look awful. What do you think caused it?"

"I have no idea, Mike. I was very sick and vomiting before I went to sleep, but I don't think anything I ate was the cause of it."

When she got to the hospital, they gave her shots to counteract the poisoning, and soon found she had been poisoned on her arthritis medication. They said that was the reason her chest felt so tight, and she was having difficulty breathing, she was swelling inside as bad as outside. She had to take shots and medication six weeks to overcome the poisoning. She had never itched so badly or had so many bright red whelps all over her body before. The palms of her hands and the bottom of her feet hurt so badly when they would whelp up from the poisoning. The wheps would disappear and she would feel fairly well, then all at once, for seemingly no reason at all, they would swell up again and itch like mad.

Tacky and Colt had just got to where they could go to Church again, and get out a little, when one morning shortly after breakfast, he began having trouble breathing. He felt like his chest was in a vice. He went outside to see if he could breathe better in the fresh air.

Tacky told him she was calling the doctor. He said, "It is just those strawberries I ate for breakfast, there is no need of bothering a doctor."

"I'd rather take you to the hospital with indigestion as to have you die with a heart attack and do nothing about it." She reasoned, and called his doctor. He was on the way to

the hospital, so she got Colt in the car and drove him to
the hospital. They immediately put him in the intensive care
unit.

A few days later they put him in a private room, and he
had company and that evening he had another heart attack.

A week later they told Tacky they were going to put him
in a private room again with restricted visitation, as soon
as she returned from lunch.

She was certainly looking forward to this for she was
having lots of back trouble again. She had stayed at the
hospital so much, and her back was acting up. She could
stand, or walk without severe pain, but she could not sit.
Anytime she sat more than ten or fifteen minutes she would get
muscle spasms running down her legs. She thought if he was put in
a private room, she could have a cot in there where she could
lie down or be up walking and help see after him.

When she returned from lunch, he had had another heart
attack. As soon as they got him stabilized again they sent him by
ambulance to Brookwood Hospital South of Birmingham. Tacky
had to lie down on the bench in the ambulance as they went to
Brookwood.

Colt said, " Honey, you're in worse shape than I am."

"I am fine as long as I don't have to sit more than a
few minutes," she said.

Wyman and Kat followed them down there, and as soon
as they got there he rented the last room the hotel in the
hospital had. Tacky said, "Why don't you wait to see if he
is put in ICCU or a private room? I won't need the hotel
room if he is put in a private room."

"Then the room might be gone." He said, "and there is
no way you can wait in the waiting room again."

A man walked up to get a room just as he had rented the

last one.

They did put Colt in ICCU, and Wyman and Kat went
home. The next day they came back with Tacky's Hip Traction.
She hooked it up on the hotel bed, and would lie in it until
visiting hours in ICCU. It sure did help. She appreciated
Wyman and Kat's thoughtfulness.

The next day they did an arteriogram on Colt and found
that he had dead muscles around the heart, but the arteries
could be treated with medication.

He was released a week later. They came home and Tacky
began working out in the garden. Her leg began hurting. She
went to the doctor. He did a biopsy and found she had
Melanoma Cancer. The doctor had to do more surgery to be sure he
got it all. She was on crutches for sometime. It was harder for
her to walk on crutches than she remembered, but the reason
was that she had to do the walking with her crippled leg, for
it was her good leg that she had the cancer in. Her crippled
foot not working in the ankle made it hard to use the crutches.

Nineteen eighty-two had been a very hard year as it had been
first one then the other for the whole year. But they were so
thankful that each had been able to help the other most of the
time.

Tacky

CHAPTER TWENTY-SEVEN

Nineteen eighty-three was a much better year. Colbert and
Tacky began to heal from their problems and gain new strength.

In July of 1984, Alvie and Rita, Colbert and Tacky's lovely
neighbors and friends bought a new van and they all planned a trip
out West. They loaded the Van down with fresh vegetables and
canned goods and made their first real stop in San Antonio, Texas
to visit a couple of days with their daughter. They strung and
broke beans for her after they got there to put in the freezer.
She was so happy to get some of mother and dad's good home grown
vegetables.

They visited the Alamo, and drove around for Alvie to see
some of the crops down around Corpus Christi.

From there they went to Paint Rock, Texas and spent a couple
of days with Colbert's niece and family, down on Concho River.
They enjoyed wandering through the pecan orchards along the river.
There were many wild fowl and animals that could be seen at
different times of the day, which Tacky and Colbert thoroughly
enjoyed. The Mexican Hats, and Indian Blankets and many other
wild flowers in that region were a beauty to behold.

After leaving Concho River, they headed west on highwy 10.
There were such beautiful mountain regions along Stockton,

Tacky

Van Horn, Sierra Blanca, and in Western New Mexico and
Eastern Arizona. They enjoyed the drive around and through
Salt River Canyon, and White Mountains. Then they spent a
day in the Painted Desert and the Petrified Forest.

Tacky marveled time and time again at the awesome beauty that
only God could create. The Proghorn Deer and the little Prairie
Dogs midst the awesome colors in the rock formations made an
unforgetable impression on Tacky's sensitive mind. She had never
seen such incredible beauty, and her mind wandered back to
Colbert's remark, "I want to show you the beauties God has created
for us to enjoy!" She thanked God for His beauties and for giving
her Colbert to enjoy them with.

She thought of the great changes in her life. After Cran's
sudden death she had to go on as though nothing had happened, but
something had happened; she could no longer say, "Go ask your
Daddy, or Daddy might let you go to town with him." It was all
up to her, every single decision. Not just the decisions 'to or
not to.' The family depended on her to set the pace for each day.
She was a person herself with needs for encouragement and inner
strength of her own, but she had to be strong for her family.
When they were blue and missing their daddy, she had to be extra
cheerful. It was no longer a time of a frivolous or serious
side of her personality, but a valuable defense against
depression and gloom. Life goes on and the children must never be
forced by her actions to feel they had been cheated out of
what other children were blessed with. So she did her best,
and they all survived.

Yes, Colbert had certainly made a big change in her life.
Every day was filled to the upmost with joys beyond her fondest
dreams.

They went to the Grand Canyon, enjoying all the beauty
they could see around the edges, then took a Canyon Tour by

Plane down into the Canyon. Tacky never knew rocks could be
so huge and so elegant in color and shape. Thunder River was
a spectacular sight, and the Colorado River with the many rafts on
it was a sight to behold. They took many pictures to write about
for their Memory Book.

Alvie enjoyed seeing the farmland with its cotton fields,
grape vineyards and other crops, down in the Imperial Valley near
Yuma. All the irrigation rigs were impressive to watch and see
what could be done with desert land.

In Escondido, California, they visited Tacky's brother and
family, her nephews and niece for a day or two, then they drove
on over to Vallejo and visited Colbert's niece and family. They
drove them all over San Francisco, showing them the different
places of interest.

They enjoyed the ride up highway 101 along the Coast through
the Redwood Forest.

They stopped in Orick, California and went to Church in a
little Baptist Church in the middle of August, but it was so cold,
they had a fire in a big coal heater, and there were only fifteen
present that Sunday morning.

They visited Alvie's niece and family in Vancouver,
Washington for several days. They took them to Multmomah Falls,
picnicking, and up to Mt. Hood. It was snow covered. Jason,
their little five-year-old son, called the men, "No Fun Men"
because they wouldn't climb over the mountain and play in the snow
with him.

The next day they all drove up to Mt. St. Helen's. This
was after the eruption, and the trees looked like toothpicks,
they were so barren of limbs or foliage. The mountainsides were
covered with the most beautiful fire flowers. It was amazing how
quickly a completely barren area could be so prominent with these
beautiful flowers again. It just seemed that God must have

sprinkled the whole area with these magnificent colors to restore His beauty to the world.

Tacky thought, 'there is never lack of hope, for even in the most tragic circumstance, God can bring so much transcendent beauty back into life.'

The snow-capped peaks of Mt. Adams and Mt. Rainier were a sight to behold. They enjoyed picking blackberries for a pie and some jam at Bayfield Lake County Park.

The next day they all enjoyed a picnic at Moulton Falls, near Basket Flats, Washington, and a ride on the Chelatchie Prairie Special.

When time came to continue their journey, it was a sad parting with such special people. They had spent a very interesting week.

They boarded a Ferry at Port Angeles, Washington for Victoria, Canada.

Colbert and Tacky enjoyed the Butchart Gardens again, as they shared points of special interest with Alvie and Rita. They had visited them in 1979 when Etheridge lived in Seattle, and they took a ferry from Seattle over to Victoria. The extreme beauty was just indescribable! The rose gardens, begonia gardens, flowering cherry trees, the bougainvillea, marigolds, dahlias, the sunken gardens, chinese garden, arbavitas and flowers of every name, color and description were growing in such gorgeous arrangements over acre after acre of beauty.

Driving back into the U.S. The International Peace Arch on highway five was a sight to see. Tacky liked the signs, "Brothers dwelling together in unity," on one side and "Children of a Common Mother," on the other side.

Yellowstone National Park held some beautiful sights for these weary, yet enthusiastic travelers. The beautiful hot springs and geysers, the elk with their huge antlers, deer, wolves and bears all so elegant, yet scary. Big Horn Pass with its many U turns was very startling at times, but held a magnificent beauty of its own. They enjoyed seeing herd after herd of Buffalo as they came into Wyoming. A great thrill in Cody, Wyoming was going to a Rodeo. The weather was so warm that day and as soon as the sun went down the temperature dropped and the icy winds came in and even with their coats and a blanket they were still cold, but the joy of the Rodeo overcame the coldness.

Mt. Rushmore was another great thrill. Then on to Kansas City, Missouri, a visit with Alvie's brother, brother-in-law and several nieces was the topping treat for the trip. It had been a great two months!

Tacky marveled at the many beautiful trips she had been privileged to make since she and Colbert married. But whether she was on a trip or working with the regular duties around home, life was filled with the joy and romance of living and loving, and being loved and blessed beyond measure!

Her young days of love and romance had been exciting and stimulating, giving splendor and fulfillment to her country girl life. Raising three wonderful children had certainly been a great challenge, and a tremendous experience, but after they were all grown and involved in their families or careers, life would have been different for Tacky. She had always been happiest when she felt needed, and when Colbert came into her life, she felt that she could fill a need in his life, as well as enrich her own with his tender love, thoughtfulness and humor.

Tacky

CHAPTER TWENTY-NINE

In 1994 Margo was taking tea out of the microwave at eleven o'clock just befor retiring for bed. The bowl slipped and spilt boiling tea in her lap. She jerked her pants down and the flesh came off with it. She rolled to their bedroom and woke Rocky up and asked him to look at her stomach.

He said "Good Lord, Margo we've got to get you to the hospital immediately. You have terrible burns." He jerked his clothes on and rolled her to the car. She couldn't get in from the passenger side without tearing off much more burned area.

"I'll have to drive," she said. They got her in the car and took off. Before she got to Hwy. 67 about a quarter of a mile from home her feet and legs were spasming so badly they were kicking the car, and Rocky tried to hold them down with all his might. By the time they got to the hospital, her whole body was going into spasms. He rushed her in, and they checked her and called an ambulance to take her to the Burn Center in Birmingham. Her temperature was so high and her body was spasming so badly, they sprayed her down with cool water and gave her a shot to try to calm her body down.

Next morning Rocky called Tacky to tell her about Margo's accident, and said, "Shayne's phone is out of order and she should be at work about now, will you please let her know?"

Tacky called Shayne, who was very upset. "Nana, are you going down?"

"Yes, just as soon as I can get ready."

"I'll get off work and go with you. I'll be out there just as quick as I can make it."

When they found out about it at work, they wouldn't let Shayne drive. One of the other girls drove her out to Nana.

It was unbelievable how severely Margo was burned. All over her stomach the tops of her legs and between her legs where the boiling tea collected. For over two weeks, Rocky wouldn't leave her. He stayed at the hospital day and night. Finally, he allowed Tacky to come down and stay with her a few days so he could go back and work some, but he was right back on the weekend. They would scrape her body down every day, which was very painful. They made pictures and studied them. Even though she was in terrible pain, she said to her doctor one day when they were scraping all the infected flesh off. "Doc, do you think I might sell these pictures to Playboy Magazine?" The doctor just cracked up with laughter.

The nurse that was helping, said, "Margo, how in the world can you think of joking when you are in such terrible pain?"

She said, "Well, you've got to think of something besides all the pain you are going through."

They had to cut so much flesh off the sides and backs of her legs to graft on the tops and inside of her legs and her stomach, that it left her hips without much padding.

After she healed, she was able to begin doing her housework again. Getting in and out of the bed and the car, bumping her hips, caused bursas to form, which began to drain. They put her

on very high doses of intravenous antibiotics every six hours day
and night. It just kept getting worse. They put a port in her
shoulder and let her go home from the hospital, but she had to
continue the strong intravenous antibiotics every six hours day
and night for three months and it just kept getting worse. They
sent her to an orthopedic doctor. He told her if she didn't have
surgery, it would kill her, and if she did, it might be worse.
Tacky went with her, and on the way home she said, "Mother, what
are we going to do?"

"Margo, when we get home I want you to call Dr. Stokes and
see what he recommends."

"But Mother, he is not doctoring anymore, he has retired."

"That doesn't matter. He was your doctor for twenty-three
years, and I'm sure he wouldn't mind you calling him at home."

She did call him as soon as she got home, and he told her the
orthopedic doctor was absolutely right, but this type of surgery
involved so much more than the bone that no matter how good the
orthopedic was he wouldn't trust one to do the surgery. He
recommended a Plastic Surgeon, and made her an appointment. When
the doctor touched the bursa on her hip it spurted pus across the
bed and ran down the wall. He said, "Good Heavens, we're going to
have to do surgery immediately. He did surgery on Monday, cutting
out a place about the size of a saucer in the hip and removing
much bone.

He said, "I had to remove so much bone and tissue, that it
will never grow flesh to cover up the hole. I will have to do
another surgery in a few days."

On Friday of that week, he took her back to surgery and cut
the muscle at the top of her knee, stripped it out up to the
groins, cut a hole through her body and pulled the muscle through,
wound it around covering the hole, and sewed it in. She had to

lie on a mattress that kept air flowing through it to help the circulation for three weeks.

Then in 2002, Margo underwent a radical mastectomy,but she still cooks and talks to sick people, teaches a Sunday School class, having the ladies out for a meal, or ice cream get together to discuss their problems. She is unable to do cosmetology any longer after her burns, but many people still come to her for counseling. She has gone through so much that she is a great help to others who are going through problems.

She and Rocky have a strong marriage, and enjoy their daughter, grandson, and a very fine son-in-law.

CHAPTER THIRTY

Tacky and Colbert's love for the wonderland of nature has
never waned. Even though they are no longer able to climb
the hills and hollows as they did in the early years of marriage,
they still get a thrill from just walking through parks and
forests. Noccalula Falls, National, Warrior and Bankhead Forests
hold precious memories, and they make it a point to continue
visiting them as often as possible.

Tacky thinks of the great courage Colbert has shown in
going through such adversities during and after Tina's death.
Then having to give up reading and driving after the loss of
his front vision, was no easy trial to accept for a person
who enjoyed independence as much as he did. Then, it was difficult
having to depend upon someone to drive him everywhere he needs or
wants to go. He is not even able to read large print with a
magnifying glass...it's all been like a nightmare that never seems
to end.

He passed out while walking recently. A neighbor saw him
fall and called 911. After several months of tests he was
diagnosed with various ailments, including: leukemia, bone marrow
cancer, two bulging disks in the lumbar spine, a tumor on the

spine, a cyst on the left kidney and gallstones, besides the
arthritis and heart problems and blindness he already had. Since
it is now only a few months until Birthday ninety. He decided not
to take the chemo, or radiation, since the medications would not
go well with his heart medicine.

Tacky had the knee on her good leg replaced in 1997, and had
to have shoulder surgery in 2001. She broke her crippled foot,in
March of 2003 and had to wear a broken foot boot for more than
four months, this spring; then, she could not wear the shoes and
brace for the foot had made a change. Special shoes have had to
be made again and attached to the brace so she can walk.

Tacky and Colbert have learned, however, as the Lord said,
"There will be trials and tribulations in this world, but be of
good cheer, I have overcome the world." So they say, "if life
deals a lemon, make lemonade, for even in the bad times God can
bring some beauty, peace, and comfort, when we trust it to his
care. Tacky reads to him, and puts songs on a tape for him to
listen to and memorize so he can still sing a solo in church
occasionally. She has been so proud that his sense of humor has
never diminished. Before they married his Pastor told her,
"You'll find Colbert to be a man with a joke for every occasion."
She has certainly found this to be true!

Tacky's family continues to have difficult circumstances,
too. In October 2001, Mike had open heart surgery. He didn't have
a heart attack, but was on the verge of one. The doctors said he
had what they called a "Widow Maker"; had he had a heart attack at
the time, there would have been no way to save him. A few months
later, he had such severe back and leg pain, three specialists
performed many tests of all kinds and treatments. They said it
would take three surgeries to help his condition, and then he
might end up in a worse condition than he is now.

Tacky

A new spinal specialist told him after studying the cat
scans, MRI's and x-rays, and from his experience with the shots
and therapy, he thought if he went into the spinal area, removed
the broken piece that were floating around, and trimmed the
bulging disc, he thought that would take pressure off the other
bulging disc and stop some of the pain running down his legs. He
said Mike would never be without pain, but it would not be the
severe pain he was experiencing then. He did the surgery and he
got some relief from it. Then, other tests showed that he had a
blockage in the carotid artery in his neck which could cause a
stroke. The muscles in his neck were so strong from years of hard
manual labor that the doctors had problems performing surgery;
these muscles caused swelling in his neck and face, and numbness
in his jaw and tongue. After more than six months, he still can't
talk plainly and has numbness on that side of his neck. Then his
right kneecap locked up from torn cartilages in it, and he had to
have surgery to take care of it. He continues to have have
terrible pain in that leg and neck.

Tacky said, "Learning to adjust takes lots of faith, but God
has been such a tremendous force and help in our lives that we
can't praise Him enough. I would like to tell others who are
experiencing the pains and heartaches that life deals that God is
always there to help us through them when we truly seek HIS help.

Tacky

Tacky

She wrote this poem in 1997 to express her trust.

GOD'S LOVE

There are many things in this life we don't understand
Mind boggling events the heart can't comprehend
But, one thing of which we can be sure
God's Love for us is sincere and pure.
When we study His Word each day,
And by His teachings are guided along the way,
Even though the path may be hard to climb,
He will give us joy and peace of mind.

His love and care,
Overshadow anything we're called to bear.
So in our heartaches, pain and strife,
When we are encumbered with the trials of this life,
May we go to Him in Trust and Prayer
Realizing the pains we are called to bear
Are nothing to compare
With the Glory we'll share over there!

"He will always give you all you need from day to day if you
will make the Kingdom of God your primary concern."
Luke 12:31 Living Bible

Tacky

DO YOU EVER WONDER WHY?

Do you ever wonder why?
Troubles so often come your way,
It seems all you can do is cry,
For the trials keep mounting day by day…

You try so hard to banish all fear and doubt
And try to understand what life is all about.
But it is only through the study of God's Word
That you will understand His unfailing concern Even for a bird.…

Then you come to realize
Many of the problems are from being unwise
And not going to Him in trust and prayer,
Casting them all unto His loving care!

For when you release them into God's Hands
Striving to fit your life into His plans
Then the peace you are seeking, you will find,
Bringing joy, fulfillment and peace of mind!

"For the Lord giveth wisdom; out of His mouth cometh knowledge and understanding."
Proverbs 2:6
By: Eloise Y. Lott

Tacky

LORD LET ME BE A CHANNEL OF YOUR LOVE

Lord please use this humble life of mine
To be a channel through which I may help
Others Your love to find.
Help me to be true to You each day,
That I might help someone find "The Way."

I know it's asking a lot Dear Lord,
For I so often stumble and fall,
But I do pray that something in my life
Will point others on Whom to call,
To find help in their struggles and strife.

For temptations are always near
Help us to meet them without fear
Knowing joy and peace only You can Give,
As through a sinful world we live.

"My son if sinners entice thee consent thou not.
My son, walk not thou in the way with them.
Refrain thy foot from their path."

Prov. 1:10
By: Eloise Y. Lott 1976

Printed in the United States
214506BV00002B/2/P

9 781607 913474